"I've had the pleasure of calling Grant Wilkins my friend and mentor for over thirty years. He is a modest, passionate, pioneer and champion of Rotary's initiative to eradicate polio. A person who has walked with kings without losing the common touch, Grant has been an inspiration to generations of Rotarians around the world. His contributions to building communities and bridging continents have benefited thousands across the globe. His impact on health, hunger, water, peace, art, culture and education have made this world a much better place. He is a true renaissance man who has lived Rotary's motto of 'Service above Self.' His memoir is a testament that indeed one 'ordinary' man can make an 'extraordinary' difference in our world.

– Colorado Rotarian Bryan Cooke,
End Polio Now Zone 27 Coordinator (2012-2015)

"Few people around the world have touched the lives of so many, and remained so humble about it. From his tireless work to eradicate the scourge of polio from the face of the earth, to his advocacy of the irrefutable impact of Rotary International, Grant has used his skills of diplomacy, encouragement and persuasion to make a mark for goodness and hope. In this writing, he shares the important lessons for success with other people who are determined to make a difference. I am proud to call Grant a mentor, an inspiration and a friend, and thrilled that he has provided this written legacy for us in our quests."

– W. Douglas Jackson,
President and CEO of Project C.U.R.E., a non-profit which
provides medical equipment to needy communities worldwide

Two Drops that Changed the World

A Polio Survivor's Journey with Rotary International to Eradicate Polio and Promote Childhood Immunization

By C. Grant Wilkins

With Cindy Brovsky

1-13-18

To Rachel with "many thanks" for your help - with Rotary International to eradicate polio & make our world a better place. May "God Bless you" along with Bill & Melinda Gates!

Grant Wilkins

ISBN: 978-1546433163 (Paperback Edition)

Editing by Cindy Brovsky
Front cover and book design by (in)spiregraphics
Photo credits C. Grant Wilkins

Printed in the United States of America
First Printing, 2017

Published by C. Grant Wilkins
P.O. Box 3304
Littleton, Colorado 80161

Dedication

I dedicate this book to the more than 1.2 million Rotarians from 170 countries worldwide who have worked to eradicate polio from our planet. Marlene and I are honored to have played a role in that effort.

Introduction

There have been two things that have greatly impacted my life: contracting the polio virus and being a member of Rotary. In 1985, those two merged and thrust me into a fight to help eradicate the crippling disease from our world.

By early 2017, we have nearly completed the fight by vaccinating 2.5 billion children in 122 countries and knocking out the virus from all but three countries: Pakistan, Afghanistan and Nigeria where a total of 5 active cases of polio were reported. Yet, this battle and many other projects embraced by Rotary, including helping third world countries access to clean water, are ongoing.

In 1998, Marlene and I were asked to represent Rotary International at a National Immunization Day in the Ivory Coast of Africa. It was inspirational to see mothers line up with their children to get the polio vaccination.

1

I have shared my story with thousands of people over the years as I helped raise money to eradicate polio. Many in my audiences suggested that I write a book.

I went to put pen to paper shortly before my 89th birthday in 2015 when I was blindsided by a diagnosis of throat cancer. Four years earlier I successfully was treated for prostate cancer.

As my 90th year approached I began to organize my thoughts. My hope is by sharing my story others will be inspired to serve in a community service club such as Rotary, Kiwanis or Lions because these clubs have made enormous impacts in lives all over the world.

I want to summarize my story in the Introduction and give you more details in each chapter. The eradication of polio was just one of my many projects with Rotary. During my more than 47 years as a Rotarian, my second wife, Marlene, and I have traveled the world promoting world peace through other health initiatives and chartering the first Rotary club in Moscow, Russia in June 1990.

We have raised money for our home state of Colorado for at-risk youth, helped secure a $101 million federal grant to provide high-speed internet access to all Coloradans, and numerous other projects.

So, let us begin this journey.

My experience with polio is unique because it not only hit me but also my first wife.

In 1951, I was a 25-year-old father with three children ages four, 18-months, and three-months and traveled to Manhattan, Kansas on business. The community recently had a flood. By the time I returned to Denver I had fallen ill and doctors initially thought I had the flu or stomach ulcer. A spinal tap showed another dreaded diagnosis. I had bulbar polio that paralyzed my throat muscles.

An experimental tracheotomy kept me from drowning in my own saliva but I could no longer swallow or talk and was kept alive with intravenous feedings for two weeks. I was hospitalized in Colorado General Hospital at 8th and Colorado where the polio ward for adults was located. Ironically, this same hospital housed the Premature Baby Ward, and our premature baby son, Steve, who weighed 2 lbs. 5 oz. when he was born in May, had been placed in their care, and after 3 months, was still there when Diane and I were both in the Polio Ward. Across town at Children's Hospital, our middle child, Mark, was being treated for rheumatoid arthritis.

Our oldest child, Sharon, was home with my wife, Diane. Thankfully, she had help and support from her family who lived nearby.

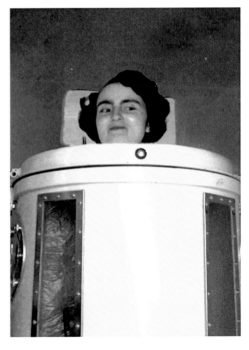

As I lay in my hospital bed in the isolation ward and watched other patients deal with paralysis and many die, I silently asked God to take me if I could not fully recover. My prayers were answered as the crisis passed and I faced months of therapy to recover my ability to eat solid food and speak.

But while I was thanking God for his mercy, my young wife fell ill. She had visited me after I was out of isolation and said she didn't feel well. Doctors immediately did a spinal tap that revealed she had the polio virus. Within 24 hours, she was paralyzed from the neck down from lumbar polio.

My first wife, Diane, lived in an iron lung in the hospital for two and a half years before we were able to bring her home with a portable chest respirator. Despite her illness, she was an inspiration for always having a smile on her face.

Once Diane was able to leave the hospital with a portable iron lung, she lived out the rest of her life in a hospital bed at our home in Denver.

Diane spent two and a half years in an iron lung in the hospital and another 11 years in a new home we built to accommodate her and her portable chest respirator.

She raised our three children from a hospital bed with the help of a live-in nurse and family members. Our extended family along with friends, doctors and nurses, other survivors of polio and their families, religious leaders and teachers at our children's schools became "our village."

"Other than the sadness I felt about my mom being in that condition, I see it as an incredibly enriched environment in which to grow up," my daughter, Shari, recalled. "It really became like a village and it was all hands on deck and everyone was around to help. We all lived within six blocks of grandparents, aunts, uncles and great-grandparents. No one gets that anymore."

It was not an easy lifestyle and at times I felt cheated from a "normal life" but Diane's upbeat, cheerful personality became legend-ary. People, including area clergy, often visited her to be inspired by her positive outlook.

When Diane passed in 1964, my life was renewed with my second wife, Marlene, my partner in life for more than 50 years. We visited 65 Rotary clubs in the West together and traveled internationally to more than 60 countries.

Marlene and I married on my birthday, October 23, 1965 but it wasn't until 1969 that I was finally in a position to carry on my father, Clarence Wilkins', longtime service as a faithful Rotarian. He had the distinction of belonging to five of the original 100 Rotary Clubs.

How did he accomplish that? Well, he was an entrepreneur who moved quite a bit and his jobs brought his family from Fort Worth, Texas, where I was born in 1926 to Oklahoma City; Lafayette, Louisiana; Omaha and Lincoln, Nebraska; and Denver. He joined the Rotary club in each of those cities.

After Diane's death, I was very fortunate to marry Marlene on Oct. 23, 1965, which happened to also be my birthday. I always tell people she was brave to take on me and three teenagers.

During our more than 50 years of marriage, Marlene and I have traveled the world with Rotary International and our own adventures. We've had a wonderful life together.

When I joined the Rotary Club of Denver my father sponsored me and we later sponsored my younger brother, Jim.

The Rotary Club of Denver had 625 members and was one of the largest in the country before satellite clubs began in all corners of the city. By 2016, the original Denver club had shrunk to about 240 members but there are 40 other clubs in the Denver metropolitan area.

"I think that Grant has brought in more new members to Rotary in the Denver area than any other person – by far," said my brother, Jim, who served as president of the Rotary Club of Denver from 1994-1995 and Denver Rotary Club Foundation president from 2003-2004. "He's such an advocate for Rotary. Everyone he meets he asks, 'Why are you not in Rotary?' Come and visit our club. He's very much enthused and a good ambassador for Rotary. He walks the talk."

I was elected president of the Rotary Club of Denver in 1978-79; Governor of District 5450 in 1984-85; and director of Rotary International in 1993-1995, for a two-year term, one of only 18 in the world. Along the way I signed up more Paul Harris Fellows in a single year than any other District Governors; helped charter new Rotary clubs in Russia; chaired the Health and Hunger Task Force for Rotary International; and started the Russian Health Initiative and Russian Health Fairs, patterned after Denver's 9Health Fair.

In 1981, I founded Artists of America – a yearly event that showcased top artists – and raised more than $3 million for the Rotary Club of Denver and the Colorado History Museum.

"Grant gets a lot done," Jim said. "I'm very proud of him and his family is very proud of what he has accomplished in Rotary. He's a crusader and whatever he gets involved in he is driven."

In 1985 when Rotary International announced the beginning of the PolioPlus campaign, it made a perfect fit that I serve on their original

PolioPlus Fundraising Committee and I continue to serve on the Polio-Plus Advocacy Committee and History Review Committee.

Rotary International's initial goal in 1985 was to raise $120 million and I began telling other Rotarians about my journey with polio. By 1988, Rotary had raised $247 million for PolioPlus – and the largest amount raised by one club came from the Rotary Club of Denver with $526,902.

"I happened to join Rotary specifically because of Grant and the speech I heard him give about PolioPlus when I was a guest at the Rotary Club of Denver," recalls Rotarian John Klug. "He was one of the early movers and shakers to get the eradication effort started in the Rotary world."

As a testament to their meaningful work, in 2016 — with the help of over 1 million Rotarians and over $1.6 billion in raised funds — there were only 37 cases of polio worldwide.

Rotary also successfully lobbied the U.S. Congress and other donor governments worldwide to pledge more than $7.2 billion toward the vaccinations. The cause has been aided by the Bill & Melinda Gates Foundation has given more than $2 billion to the cause and partnerships with the World Health Organization (WHO), UNICEF and the Centers for Disease Control and Prevention (CDC).

Those combined efforts have allowed volunteers – including Rotarians - to immunize more than 2.5 billion children age 5 and under in 122 countries. Marlene and I had the life-changing experience of helping to vaccinate children in the Ivory Coast in Africa.

Marlene's photograph was taken as she was giving one child two drops of the vaccine, which has been published in several Rotary marketing items about PolioPlus.

"I call that trip a 'goose bump' experience," Marlene said. "The photo where I am putting "two drops" of polio vaccine into the baby's mouth shows how pleased the mother was as she pushed her way through the

Marlene described our participation at a National Immunization Day in the Ivory Coast of Africa as a "goose bump moment." This photo of her giving a child the polio vaccination was used on many Rotary marketing brochures.

crowds of people up to me, and made sure that her child would be immunized. It was a moving experience for me as this precious baby grabbed my arm."

With great joy, we have watched regions of the world become polio-free with polio cases reported primarily in the countries of Afghanistan and Pakistan where immunization has been thwarted by the Taliban. It was reported that the Taliban in those two countries had killed 80 polio immunization volunteers since 2001.

It would be amazing to see polio eradicated in my lifetime. I also am hopeful that Rotary will begin even more clean water projects in the coming years to deal with that issue, which causes more deaths daily than polio at its worst. As of mid–April 2017, there are only five cases of polio in the world. To date, polio eradication has saved 2.5 billion children and 16 million children have been saved from paralysis caused by polio.

"I think what has impressed me the most about Grant is that he just wants the best for other people," said Rotarian Steve Werner of Denver. "Rotary has given him the opportunity to provide service to people around the world. He is just a very compassionate person."

Another area I feel needs more education is the importance of immunization in the United States. With each generation removed from the polio epidemic that ravaged our country from the late 1800s until Jonas Salk's groundbreaking vaccination in 1955, followed by Albert Sabin's oral vaccination in 1961, there is a lack of education about the need to immunize children here.

My home state of Colorado has one of the worst immunization rates in the country, although new laws passed in 2014 make it harder for parents to opt their children out of vaccinations. We've had measles outbreaks in the public schools because a parent's decision not to immunize affects all children in the community.

Former President of Rotary International Jim Lacy, who served as national coordinator for the PolioPlus campaign and chairs the advocacy committee, says the United States is just one plane ride away from another possible polio outbreak if American parents fail to vaccinate their children.

"Someone can fly in here from some other part of the world that has polio and start this all over again," Lacy said. "Grant and I have both been doing this since 1985… I just am absolutely amazed at where we started and where we are today. We are going to eradicate polio and we just have to keep plugging; we just can't stop now. We spent too much money, too much time and effort and we have to finish the job."

Rotary's motto is "Service Above Self" and I believe I have lived that creed throughout my work in Rotary. Additionally, among my many civic activities I have worked with the alumni at the University of Denver, served on the Swedish Medical Center Board of Directors and Mesa Verde National Park Foundation Board of Directors.

My daughter, Shari, and son, Mark, will share their memories through-out the book. Sadly, my youngest son, Steve, passed away suddenly from a heart attack at age 47 in 1999.

Mark was asked about my legacy. The question caught him off guard. Initially, he said he was proud that as a business owner I was willing to give people down on their luck a job. Mark worked for me in our sign business first at age 13 doing odd chores and then running his own crew putting up billboards when he was in high school and college.

"Some of the people he hired had gone to jail or were alcoholics or people who just needed a second chance," Mark recalled. "And he would give them a second chance. Often times he would be disappointed but he still gave them the opportunity. So, I guess when I see what he's done with polio it is once again giving people a second chance at life."

A week after that visit Mark sent an email elaborating on my legacy. I think it sums up why I hope my story will inspire others and why I am writing this book.

"When you asked this question it threw me for a loop," Mark wrote. "What I see is a man that has always tried to do the right thing. He faced his challenges head on and did the best he could to make it all work out for the greater good."

Mark teaches middle school in Fairfield, Iowa and his "Science of Creative Intelligence" class includes 16 basic principles including, "seek the highest first."

"I believe my father embodies that principle," Mark wrote. "He stood by my mother through very hard years, he gave people a second chance when he could, he was a big brother through (Rotary), he raised money for an organization that promoted world peace and service above self, and he had a major impact in the elimination of polio. And still he keeps going, working on the clean water project and there will be others for as long as he is capable. He is on a 'hero's journey'. And all of this he has done humbly, never trying to draw attention to his self."

Mark continues: "His reward has been the satisfaction of knowing that he has done something to make the world a better place, truly service above self. He may not be recognized in history books, but his impact will be felt by many people for generations. That is what I think his legacy is. Also, you cannot overlook the role that Marlene played. They are a team, and her love and support behind the scenes has helped in every project they undertook. It is a bond of love that has sustained, nourished and driven them to accomplish so much."

What better rewards than to have your child write something like that? As long as I am able, I will continue to be active with Rotary, DU, and my community at large. I hope my story encourages other to do the same in their communities and the world.

Original 1985 Polio Committee at Rotary International Headquarters
From left to right, front row: Pratt Secrest, Cliff Dochterman, Herb Brown, Don Kwait, Grant Wilkins and Rick King. Back row: Bob Cerwin, Ray Wells, Jack Forrest, Art Richardson and Mike Pedrick. Note: Herb Brown, Cliff Dochterman and Rick King would go on to serve as Rotary International Presidents.

I was three and a half years old and living in Fort Worth, Texas when this photo was taken with my father, Clarence. His work in Rotary inspired me to join many years later as an adult when I lived in Denver.

My middle name is Grant after my mother's maiden name, Elsie Duffel Grant. This photo was taken in 1928 when I was 2 years old.

Chapter 1

My Childhood and Father's Devotion to Rotary

A salesman who could make friends with anyone

When I was born in 1926, I was named after my father Clarence but I go by my middle name, Grant, which was my mother's maiden name. Elsie Duffel Grant was born and raised in Kansas City. She had several sisters. I was closest to my Aunt Miriam Grant who never married and later in life taught at Colorado College in Colorado Springs.

As a child, I remember me, my parents and younger brother, Jim, traveling to Kansas City to visit my mom's family on holidays. We stayed in their tiny house with one small bathroom. We didn't think anything of it because that was all they had.

My dad was born in Austin, Texas and moved to Oklahoma City where my grandfather James Wilkins was a traveling shoe salesman. He took the train or bus to visit customers because in those days there were no interstate highways or airplanes.

My grandmother Alice "Bess" died when my father was 18 and in Europe fighting in World War I. I don't know if he was drafted by the U.S. military or volunteered. He served in the field artillery and was stationed in France.

Dad used to tell us a story about when on Christmas Eve soldiers from Germany came out with white flags and embraced the soldiers from the U.S. and France. I always thought that story was a pipe dream until I saw the movie, "War Horse," where they reenacted that exact scene. The soldiers hunkered down in trenches dug with shovels stood up and came out for a moment of peace.

We were living in Oklahoma City in 1934 when this photo was taken on my 8th birthday.

Mother graduated from Kansas University and was a classmate of Walt Disney. She didn't know him well but she knew who he was. I believe her degree was in journalism. Dad went to Oklahoma University where his folks were living after the end of WWI. He went to OU for two years and dropped out to go to work in the oil fields.

I'm not exactly sure how my parents met but one story I recall is they were set up on a blind date. Mom was living with her folks in Kansas City, Missouri and dad's folks lived in Mexico, Missouri at the time. I'm not sure why my dad was in Kansas City when he met my mom. It was something I never asked them. But I know after they got married on Christmas Eve they got on a train for their honeymoon and went to Fort Worth, Texas where dad's new job was located.

I was born in Fort Worth where dad was in the feed and grain business. He was a member of the local Rotary club in Fort Worth and quickly joined the Rotary club in Oklahoma City when we moved there when I was 4 years old.

In Oklahoma City, he managed a national brokerage firm now called Merrill Lynch but in those days was called Fenner & Beane. That job lasted from 1930 to 1937 when he got an offer to work as a retail marketer for Continental Oil in Lafayette, Louisiana. He helped build service stations where motorists filled up with Conoco gas, and his business also delivered oil and grease to drilling rigs in Louisiana. He was kind of a pioneer in that business as more motorized cars were sold, and of course he joined the local Rotary club in Lafayette where he would serve as president in 1943-1944.

My earliest memory of my father's activities in Rotary was the local club's work with a local orphanage. The Rotarians had a Christmas party for the orphans and I believe we also would take food to the orphanage. This was before local Rotary clubs were involved in international projects. Instead, they focused on how they could help their local community.

My first taste of community service was through the Boy Scouts in Louisiana and I became an Eagle Scout. I was the first Boy Scout in Louisiana to earn the top three merit badges: bronze, silver and gold palms. Boy Scouts helped fill my free time and taught me leadership skills at a young age.

We stayed in Lafayette through my high school years and the climate and racism were a shock to me. This was long before air conditioning so we had to get creative on how we could cool off. I remember when one of my mother's sisters would come visit, my mom would get a 50-to-100-pound block of ice, put it in a huge pan, set it on the floor in front of a fan and she and my aunt would gather together and cool off. I and my brother, Jim, who is four years younger than me, often would head to the

I was very active in the Boy Scouts when we lived in Louisiana. In 1942, my parents stood behind me (far left) when I got my Eagle Scout awards.

15

I was only 16 years old when I graduated from high school in Lafayette, Louisiana. In those days, the Louisiana education system stopped at the 11th grade.

local swimming pool to get relief from the heat and humidity.

One year, Lafayette got 24 inches of rain in 24 hours and we navigated the flooded city in my dad's fishing boat.

The city's population was primarily French Canadians, known as Cajuns, who were Roman Catholic. So, I was the only Protestant in my class of about 30 students. Throughout our time there, we often attended weddings and funerals at St. John Cathedral – the main Catholic Church in Lafayette, which remains my favorite church building. On the grounds is a 500-year-old oak tree, which has a trunk with the diameter of 9-feet, 2-inches.

I graduated from high school when I was 16 because the Louisiana education system stopped at the 11th grade. The summer after high school graduation I entered Southwestern Louisiana Institute, now the University of Louisiana at Lafayette. I remember that summer very well because we'd sit in those unbearably hot classrooms and leave a pool of sweat in our wake.

The racism in Lafayette also made me very uncomfortable. The discrimination against blacks was unbelievable. They were half of the population but they had only one rundown school that wasn't the size of a modest home. Many blacks couldn't read or write. The majority lived in houses without windows or indoor plumbing.

Many blacks worked as maids and cooks. We hired a black woman who arrived at our home every morning at 7 a.m. to cook breakfast, clean the house and cook our main meal before leaving around 1:30 p.m. or so. I think my folks paid her something like 30 cents an hour, which added up to about $1.50 a day or about $7.50 a week. She also had what we called "tote" privileges and could take all the leftover food she could carry each day. To get an idea of what the cost of living was at that time in history, gasoline cost 10 cents a gallon and movies were 25 cents.

Previously when we lived in Oklahoma City a Native American woman lived with us and provided similar services. I never felt superior to the minorities in the cities I lived in, and later in life I would culti-

I was the only Protestant in my class of about 30 students in Lafayette, Louisiana. But one of my favorite buildings is St. John Cathedral – the main Catholic Church in Lafayette, which is more than 100 years old. On the grounds is a 500-year-old oak tree, which has a trunk with the diameter of 9-feet, 2-inches.

vate friendships with blacks and Native Americans from various tribes. One of my oldest and best friends was Navajo Roger Davis of Window Rock, Arizona.

After my first year of college in 1944, my father found another business opportunity in Denver where I would live the majority of my life. He became the sales manager for the Colorado Milling and Elevator Company, which produced Hungarian flour among other things. The company was headquartered in Denver and dad was hired as the southeastern sales manager. That meant he had to travel a lot by train to Georgia and other parts of the southeast.

17

My parents, Clarence and Elsie, moved to several cities throughout their marriage but came back to Denver, Colorado after my wife, Diane, and I were stricken with polio.

"It was hard to lose all of your friends and start over," my brother, Jim, recalled of moving. "But it also taught us how to make new friends. So the minus side is you lose a lot of old friends but the plus side is you learn to make new friends."

I was absolutely excited to trade the heat and humidity of Louisiana for the Colorado mild summers. My parents bought a home in an area known as Park Hill and my brother entered Smiley Junior High School while I transferred any credits I could to the University of Denver.

I'd drive my car down a gravel road - South Colorado Boulevard now one of Denver's busiest arterial roads - to get to the campus. There also was a street car that stopped at DU, which is why we called it Tramway Tech.

I had a 1936 Ford that you could still crank when the battery went dead. One way I was able to buy insurance and maintain that car was working a summer job with one of our neighbors, a character named Will Birkenmayer, who also was a DU student. We headed to the mountains and worked blasting a trail from the top of Mount Evans parking lot to the top of the peak. We drilled holes in huge rocks and then crews would blast them apart. We did that for awhile that summer but it was rough carrying heavy equipment at 14,000 feet. So, the rest of the summer I spent working at Estes Park at a resort called the Dark Horse.

The Dark Horse had a bar, dance hall and swimming pool and I was hired to be a life guard. Not a bad switch from busting rocks to sitting in the sun watching the swimmers. The job included nearby housing, which was a dilapidated cabin built over the Big Thompson River. There were so many holes in the wooden floor that I could see the river roll under the cabin from inside.

Once school started in the fall, I also made a little money by starting a carpool to DU with students in my neighborhood, including my buddy Will. I picked them up and they pitched in something like 50 cents a person for gas.

I joined the Beta Theta Pi fraternity at DU right away to make new friends at my new college. They had a nice fraternity house, which was occupied by R.O.T.C. students during World War II, but I lived with my parents for a couple of years. My folks often visited Estes Park on the weekends and I'd invite my fraternity buddies over for parties. Usually, they were pretty calm get-togethers and my parents were never the wiser.

But one weekend there was a football game between DU and Utah University. I invited our Beta fraternity brothers from Utah to join our local frat brothers for a party. We weren't wild and no women were there but we were college students and drinking beer.

When a beer bottle was empty some partiers lined up the bottle on our outdoor fancy ornamental fence. By the end of the party, there were beer bottles between each of the fence spikes. After the party broke up some friends helped me retrieve the bottles and other trash before my folks got home. I thought I was in the clear but I failed to look at the ceiling. Some of the Utah frat brothers were tall and they thought it was funny to peel the beer bottle labels and throw them on the ceiling, where they stuck and were in full view when my parents came home.

As I mentioned, my dad was the only Rotarian we know who belonged to five of the first 100 Rotary clubs: Fort Worth, Texas; Oklahoma City; Denver, Colorado; Omaha, Nebraska; and Lincoln, Nebraska. He also was a member and president of the Rotary club in Lafayette but that wasn't one of the first 100 clubs.

He was unique because other families didn't move around like we did, nor did men join that many original clubs in a lifetime.

The Rotary Club of Denver has a deep history. In 1911, seven Denver men founded Club 31 whose parent was the original Rotary Club of Chicago and Rotary International. Chicago attorney Paul Harris founded Rotary in 1905 as a way to gather business leaders weekly to network and help their city.

Harris had a connection to Denver, which author Rosemary Fetter, details in the book "The First 100 Years, Denver Rotary Celebrates a Century of Service." Harris' parents spent their later years in Denver and Harris as a young man worked as an actor at a local theater, a reporter at The Denver Post and Denver Times and as a cowboy on a ranch in northern Colorado, she wrote.

While there was no shortage of men's clubs in Denver in 1911, Club 31 founder Gratton E. Hancock wanted a group whose focus was community service. The 39-year-old manager for the Smith-Premier Typewriter Company even promoted Rotary on his business card to attract new members.

In addition to Hancock, the original members of the Denver club were a businessman, a curio shop owner, an architect, an attorney, a business school secretary and a hotel manager.

Some of the first members had already been involved with Denver Mayor Robert Speer's "City Beautiful" project, an ambitious plan to improve the city's appearance. Many of those projects remain today with well-groomed city parks, tree-lined thoroughfares, and Civic Center at the heart of city and state government buildings. Members lobbied the legislature for more money to improve roads and highways statewide. The warden of the state penitentiary agreed to use prisoners for free labor on the roadwork.

Denver Rotarians also worked to help the poor, homeless and war veterans. By 1921, Club 31 had sponsored clubs statewide and in Wyoming and New Mexico. Colorado governors, mayors and other notables became club members and helped mold the future of the city and state.

There was an attempt by Denver Rotarians in 1925 to bring the Rotary International Convention to Estes Park and that failed when they couldn't raise enough money to build an auditorium to seat 4,000. But the group landed the 1926 convention for Denver and then raised $80,000 to expand an 1889 hotel and rename it the Cosmopolitan. The expanded hotel near downtown Denver opened just in time for the convention.

Denver would host other Rotary International conventions over the years, and Denver Rotarians met in that hotel for many years before the hotel wanted the space for other paying events. Club 31 moved the weekly meetings to the Denver Athletic Club where we still meet today.

My dad wasn't able to join Rotary when my family relocated here in 1944 but he would become a member of Club 31 in December 1958.

As I mentioned, my dad liked new job opportunities and by 1946 he moved my mom and brother to Omaha, Nebraska to head up the office of Harris Upham, a stock brokerage firm. By 1953, dad was packing up my mom and brother again and they moved to Lincoln, Nebraska where he went to work for an outdoor advertising company called Western Goodroads Service Company. They had signs and billboards along the highways advertising major oil companies, such as "Gasoline: Two Miles, Turn Right." Their plant was in Lincoln and dad enjoyed that job.

I can't remember my mother ever complaining about moving every few years. They were very social people and had friends in every town they lived. My brother, Jim, eventually would come back to Colorado and attend the University of Colorado in Boulder.

"My dad was always in sales but he moved from one thing to another," Jim recalled. "He just loved a new challenge. He never met a challenge he didn't like. To some extent Grant and I are the same way. We tend to want to solve problems, both of us in our careers and extracurricular activities."

I had no intention of leaving Denver or DU but their move meant I needed to find a new home and I moved into my fraternity house.

I enjoyed DU and initially thought I would study to be a doctor. I got a part-time job at Mercy Hospital and worked after classes from 3-7 p.m. as an orderly. I did about everything, including taking bodies to the morgue. The hospital was operated by Catholic nuns and I still remember Sister Mary Andrew. The majority of the nurses were nuns who lived in a building behind the hospital.

But the hospital also employed lay women as nurses who also lived in the same building as the nuns. I helped one of those nurses sneak out her bedroom window one night, led her to my car and we drove to a fraternity party. She wasn't supposed to leave the building after 10 p.m. but we never got caught and I got her home safely. When you're young you do crazy things.

I enjoyed the hospital work and still have an interest in medicine but my career path turned to business when I met fellow student Diane Schoelzel. The Denver native was a year behind me at DU and I wasn't sure what she was even studying, although many women at the time attended college for their "Mrs. Degree." We hit it off right away.

One of my first dates with Diane was going to Central City for an opera with her father, Charles "Charlie" Schoelzel, who was vice president of a large Denver real estate company called Van Schaack and Company. During intermission of the opera, her father took me to a nearby gambling hall and we got back after the opera already resumed and they wouldn't let us in. That was kind of embarrassing.

But I got along well with Charlie and Diane's mother, Lona, and her siblings: Elaine "Laini", Phil and Wesley. They would all play a major role in our marriage and our children's lives.

Diane and I got married my senior year at DU, which was pretty common in those days. Many students married their last year in school or the month they graduated. So, we got married, had a baby the following May and I graduated from DU in June. Talk about a major life change in a short amount of time.

Our daughter, Sharon Anne Wilkins, kept Diane busy while I started my new career as a salesman for the Colorado Potato Growers Exchange. It was a cooperative of potato growers headquartered in Denver. Our members grew Russet Burbank and Red McClure potatoes and onions in the Greeley area and San Luis Valley. We'd ship carloads of potatoes and onions all over the country. Our customers included chain grocery stores.

Before I graduated from DU, I had gotten some sales experience by working part-time at F.W. Woolworth's. And I guess I have sales in my DNA from my dad.

My job with the Colorado Potato Growers Exchange was moving along fine and our family was rapidly growing. Mark joined our family and we got another surprise when Steve arrived 15 months later. His premature birth was frightening because he was so little at 2 pounds, 5 ounces and in those days they did not quite understand what caused premature babies to go blind. They later discovered it was from too much oxygen in the incubator. Steve's eyesight was impacted but not seriously.

Doctors also were somewhat baffled by Mark's rheumatoid arthritis and they hospitalized him at Children's Hospital at the same time Steve was at Colorado General Hospital. While these medical issues were going on, I had to travel to Manhattan, Kansas for the Colorado Potato Growers Exchange. There had been a flood there and unclean standing water – a breeding ground for the polio virus – was visible throughout the city.

I hadn't really been affected much by polio growing up. I remember the swimming pools sometimes being closed when an outbreak hit a community where we were living. Parents also were afraid to let their children go to movie theaters because they thought too many kids in a closed building could spread the virus. They just didn't know how it was spread in those days and that was terrifying.

I knew Franklin Roosevelt was stricken by polio as an adult before he was elected president. I had read he went to Warm Springs, Georgia to get treatment in the natural warm springs and with hot towels. Otherwise, for me polio was just something that happened to other people.

When I returned to Denver from Manhattan, Kansas I was sick. At first I thought maybe I had the flu because I couldn't keep any food down. Doctors thought maybe it was a stomach ulcer and treated me for that for 24 hours. When I started to get worse, I went to Colorado General Hospital and that's where a doctor recommended a spinal tap.

The test showed I had contracted bulbar polio that had paralyzed my throat muscles. Polio would be the center of my young family's life and totally change my wife's life for the next 13 years.

My parents, Clarence and Elsie, had a long marriage and helped me raise my three children before Marlene and I married. We all stayed close until their deaths.

Chapter 2

Our Lives with Polio

The impact of the disease on my family

There are really no words that can accurately describe the feeling of being in an isolation ward with polio victims. My head was consumed with fear of the virus spreading from my throat and that I could become paralyzed in other parts of my body.

I heard the constant hum of the men trapped in iron lungs that allowed them to breath and watched as nurses removed the patients who died.

The doctors saved my life by performing a tracheotomy in my hospital bed in the isolation ward. They couldn't move me to an operating room for fear of spreading the polio virus to other patients. While the procedure was experimental for bulbar polio patients, they knew I could develop suffocating pneumonia if they didn't act quickly. Within two weeks, my fever had broken and I was on the road to recovery.

Months of therapy would include first relearning how to swallow liquids and then eating baby food. At age 25, I also had to learn how to speak again because my vocal cords had been paralyzed.

The doctors thought it was safe for my wife, Diane, to visit me in the hospital. Sometimes I wonder how different our lives would have been if she stayed away for longer. But she often was at Colorado General Hospital anyway to visit our premature son, Steve, who was in the same facility in the premature ward while I was in the polio isolation ward.

After I was out of the isolation ward, Diane came to visit me and she said she wasn't feeling well. The doctors put her in a room next to

My first wife, Diane, and I met while attending the University of Denver. In about 1946, we attended a Sadie Hawkins dance together.

mine and immediately performed a spinal tap. Their quick actions saved her life but everything had changed. Within 24 hours she was paralyzed by lumbar polio and placed in an iron lung. She would remain in that iron lung and in the hospital for two and half years.

"My memories are kind of spotty for those early years," said our daughter, Shari, who was four years old at the time. "My first memory of my mom in the hospital was going to visit and seeing her in the iron lung. It was like, what is this? She could still talk to me but I couldn't touch her and she couldn't touch me. So there was this kind of conflicted feeling of well I get to see her but this is different."

Shari also remembers forming friendships with the doctors, nurses and other polio victims and their families while Diane was in the hospital.

"We got to be part of a medical family on that ward," Shari said. "The nurses, the doctors and the patients we got to know kind of watched out for us."

Both of our families immediately jumped in to help with our children. Diane's sister, Elaine "Laini" came back to Denver from Seattle. She became a doctor and was close to our children until her death in 2014. Shari in particular looked at her like a second mother and was Laini's caretaker at the end of her life.

My brother, Jim, was attending CU in Boulder and came down to help when he wasn't in class. Diane's parents helped care for Shari and Mark and when Steve was released from the hospital they took him to their home where he lived for a couple of years.

I was able to leave the hospital within six weeks. My parents visited from Nebraska to help and we hired a housekeeper to give our parents and other family members some relief. It took several months of speech therapy for me to regain my voice, properly pronounce syllables and speak clearly.

"I would come down on weekends and try and help and be involved with things. It was a scary time," Jim recalled. "They didn't know what was causing polio. I remember I was in Lincoln, Nebraska that summer part of the time. I had a stiff neck, it was just a sprained neck, but mom had a doctor at that time that came to the house. He came out and he checked me for polio because he thought I may have polio, too, but I didn't."

No one is quite sure why Denver had a polio epidemic in 1951. Other waves of the virus passed through the city in the 1920s, 30s and 40s with an entire wing of Children's Hospital becoming home for recovering youth. Many young patients died and others lived at the hospital for a year or more and dealt with weakened limbs and paralysis for the rest of their lives.

Other parts of the country would get hit through the early 1950s as my fellow Rotarian John Schwandke of Chicago recalled when he visited the Rotary Club of Denver in 2016. He was 7 years old in 1953 and living in Muscatine, Iowa when stricken with polio. His parents could only look through a window at him in the isolation ward because of the fear of transmitting the virus. He spent two weeks in the hospital and three months in recovery.

"We went from literally no polio cases to getting several in that town of about 25,000," Schwandke recalled. "And it was almost like the virus came up Eighth Street where I lived because a block down the street from me a little girl got it. She was four years younger than me. Now an adult, she has a fully paralyzed leg and she still wears the old-fashioned iron brace. And of course that leg did not keep up with her healthy leg so she has a big limping gate to swing the brace. A boy a few blocks up the street from me got it and he died. Parents were afraid to let their kids play with other kids because we just didn't know how the virus spread."

Denver Rotarian John Klug, who is friends with Schwandke, has a similar story of being stricken at age seven in Lebanon, Missouri in 1952.

"I was in the hospital for about two weeks but of course it was a very difficult time for my parents because no one knew then how polio was transmitted," Klug said. "There were lots of theories but no one really knew. It could be transmitted from person to person so no one wanted to be around me. My mother was worried about my brother and sisters."

Klug was in therapy for a year and shows no residual effects of the virus.

"But there is something called post-polio syndrome and it tragically strikes about 50 years after the initial exposure to polio," Klug said. "It can have more devastating effects 50 years afterwards than it did originally."

Many polio survivors get hit with the syndrome because their muscles were weakened when the virus hit and with age the original symptoms return.

Both Klug and Schwandke have been actively working to eradicate polio through Rotary because like me they understand the devastating emotional and physical impacts on the victims and their families.

Once I was recovered from my polio and was able to travel my father suggested I join his highway sign advertising business. Diane and I were fortunate to have a major medical insurance plan that covered $100,000 in medical costs, which in those days went much further and lasted a few years. Additionally, the March of Dimes helped defray our medical costs and provided medical equipment – including a wheelchair – once Diane was able to come home. I worked for several years to raise money for the March of Dimes because of all the good that organization has done.

Diane also helped with fundraisers for March of Dimes. One year, I pushed her in her wheelchair door-to-door and we collected donations from our neighbors for a fashion show fundraiser in Denver. We helped local volunteers raise $25,000 and Diane was featured in a news article about the event.

While we weren't panicked with medical bills, I needed to get some normalcy in my life and back to work. With the comfort of knowing our families were caring for our children, I took my dad's offer and began working and traveling again. Dad was still working for the Western

Diane and I were blessed with three children: Sharon Anne "Shari", Steve and Mark.

Goodroads Service Company and hired me as a salesman for Colorado, Wyoming and New Mexico.

Then dad's entrepreneur instincts kicked in and he thought we should start our own sign company, which he named Mountain States Advertising. We purchased signs from Western Goodroads that they had in Colorado, Wyoming and New Mexico. Then we expanded to build our own double-faced signs for Mountain States Telephone Yellow Pages placed in the states of Colorado, Wyoming, New Mexico, Arizona, Utah, Montana, Idaho, North Dakota, South Dakota, Nebraska, Kansas and Oklahoma.

I still carry my Mountain States Advertising business cards in my wallet. We built and maintained the billboards, and negotiated with landowners to put up the signs on private property along major highways and all interstate highways.

Most of our signs were along interstate highways but they rested on farmland and open fields. The landowners (mostly farmers) appreciated the income because they didn't have to do anything to earn it; they just let us use their property for the signs. The fact our signs were on their land could earn them $100 a year and they didn't have to lift a finger.

Before television advertising, the main national advertising was seen on billboards that lined the highways. Because we were just starting out, I traveled quite a bit. I had several states to cover and our main customers were the major oil companies: Exxon, Conoco, Phillips and Chevron that advertised their goods and services.

The oil companies were wonderful clients because they would pay us a year in advance instead of us having to bill them. That allowed us to have capital to grow the business. But I also felt I had to give them really good service and would fly out of Denver and meet at their headquarters in Montana, Houston and El Paso. I also drove around Colorado and its neighboring states contacting local gas station owners and others to sell the signs to.

Meantime, our family adjusted to visiting Diane in the hospital for two-and-a-half years before she could come home.

"It was never a traditional family," Shari said. "Dad and his father started working in highway advertising so they were gone a lot."

Our son, Mark, has seen photographs of his mother holding him as a baby before she was stricken with polio.

"I am told that I went to the hospital to visit her but I don't remember that," Mark said. "I must have been 5 when they brought her home from the hospital and that is when I remember her well."

When the portable respirator was invented, it was a way we could bring Diane home from the hospital but we needed to build a home suitable for her to be moved from room to room in her hospital bed. We built our new home two doors away from where we lived before polio to be near my in-laws because they would be caretakers for Diane and the kids, along with hiring a full-time nurse.

"They built a house that was probably one of the first handicapped suitable homes," Mark said. "It was built around her needs being able to move her hospital bed and have a wheelchair."

The main hallway that led to the bedrooms, kitchen and dining area was wide enough for a hospital bed. "The hall was long enough that we had a shuffle board built into the tile," Shari said. "We'd play there and ride our tricycles and scooters up and down the hall. It was pretty cool."

Diane mothered our children from her hospital bed for the next 11 years. Our live-in nurse, the longest being Ruth Chrisman, or other adult family members would move Diane's bed outside of each child's room so she would speak to them at night or tell them a story when they were little. As they grew, Diane often helped the kids with their homework.

Our children didn't have a conventional childhood but Diane did the best she could being a mother to them from her hospital bed in our home. Shari, Mark and Steve (not pictured) were very close to her and impacted by her death.

Her bedroom was centrally located so she knew what was going on in the rest of the house.

"She could always hear us," Mark recalled. "She always had acute hearing. I don't know if she developed this out of necessity or if she just had good hearing. But she could hear us. At times I shared a room with my brother, Steve, and a few times we'd tried to get out of bed to get a cookie and she could hear us. I'm sure we weren't that quiet but she always heard us.

"She could monitor us and be involved in our lives from wherever she was in the house because she was in the central part of the house," Mark said.

The kids greatly respected their mother and they seldom acted out.

"Some of my friends would sneak off and do things," Shari said. "I would have never done that. It might have created some chaos and burden in our family that no one needed. So I was a Goodie-Two Shoes. I would call her and say we're going to Boulder while the rest of my friends would sneak out. I'd tell her who is driving and when I will be back. I would never have done anything to create that kind of burden."

The first portable respirator that allowed Diane to come home was pretty large. It was called a Monaghan Ventalung Respirator. She was connected to it 24-hours a day and could only talk when it was compressed.

"My brother and I thought it was a great toy," Mark recalled. "It was this giant machine with dials. But then they made a portable one that was the size of a suitcase and that allowed a lot of freedom in terms of where she could go in her wheelchair. When there were power outages, which we had occasionally, she was in trouble really quickly."

The doctors taught her how to "frog breathe" where she would inhale deeply and puff out her cheeks like a frog to keep oxygen in her lungs.

"She could do that for about 45 minutes until she was so exhausted that she couldn't do it anymore," Mark said. "But her ability to do that allowed us to take her and her wheelchair and put her in a car and drive her to my grandparents for Christmas or to church. We'd plug her in when we got there. I remember taking her to see a drive-in movie. Her ability to do that allowed her a lot of freedom. My parents went out a couple of times when I was a kid. It allowed a little bit more of normalcy."

On one of those outings I took Diane to a University of Denver football game. The college was aware of our situation and allowed us to park our car on the track field that circled the football field so Diane had a better view. But more importantly we had to plug her respirator into the car's battery so it would continue to recharge and pump air into her lungs.

Near the end of the game the respirator's battery failed to recharge and Diane began frog breathing. My only option was to start up the car, drive on the track and get her help. I drove under the stadium stands and the athletic director helped me run the electrical cord from her respirator through a window and into his office to plug it in. The adrenaline was running high but we avoided a disaster.

Our families always were by our sides and available to help. My parents eventually moved back to Denver from Nebraska and settled near our home. We had the full-time nurse but I didn't realize until writing this book how much the kids helped their mother as they grew older.

"As we got older we started taking on more responsibility for the cooking and the cleaning and the ironing," Mark recalled. "We would rotate. One of us would cook, one would clean up and one would feed mom. My dad was not there a fair amount of time because he traveled a lot for work. So the three of us would sort of negotiate this routine for cooking and other things when we were home; someone else was there during the day when we were in school. And my grandparents were close by and aunts and uncles and people in the community always helped."

"I didn't like to do the cooking," Mark said. "I always was better at cleaning up or feeding mom. We just sat in a chair and she had a tray with her food on it, and I had a tray with my food on it. I'd feed her and we talked. I don't know who showed me how to do it. I don't remember any of that but it never seemed like anything. We just did it. This is how our house ran. This was our normal."

Shari helped her grandmother with such things as dressing her mother.

"We had housekeepers and my grandmother was there every morning to help get my mom ready until I was old enough to do some of those duties," Shari said. "We were part of a village of helpers. One set of grandparents would bring dinner on Sunday nights and the other set of grandparents would bring dinner on Thursday nights."

Diane also tried to make the best of the situation by playing Scrabble with Shari and other games with the kids. She also took advantage of items developed to help disabled people so that she could read books, type letters and other items and talk on the telephone.

Her father had connections with the local telephone company and they set up speakers on Diane's hospital bed. The only limb Diane could move was the big toe on her right foot. They set up the speakers so that they were connected to a button Diane could

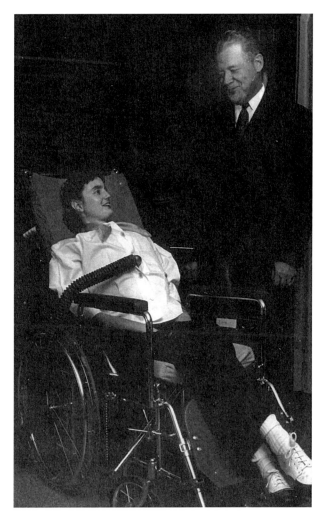

Diane often had visitors in our home, including ministers, who were inspired by her upbeat attitude.

push with her toe and get an operator. The operator would then dial the number for Diane. This was important for medical emergencies but also so that she could have daily conversations with her friends.

She was an avid reader her whole life and wasn't going to let her illness stop her from reading.

"This thing had these little clips on strings and you put one on each page and it also had a little disk that she pushed with her toe and it turned the page. It was the coolest thing. She read veraciously," Shari said.

When the first electric typewriters came out, Diane wanted one. She also painted by using her mouth to hold the paint brush.

"She learned to type when the electric typewriters first came out, with a mouth guard with a stick on it." Shari said. "She wanted to type. She typed the school directories and a lot of the church directory stuff as volunteer work. She also learned to paint that way. I have a painting that

Diane didn't have the use of her hands but that didn't stop her from learning to paint with a paint brush in her mouth. She also learned to type using another device in her mouth that would touch the keys.

she did. I think it was paint by numbers but it was done with the brush in her mouth. She found adaptations to make her life richer."
Diane did whatever she could to create a good environment for the kids.

"She raised us on music," Shari said. "We always had music playing, everything from opera to Judy Collins to folk music. It was always there so I had a great exposure to some really different kinds of music."

Mark admired his mother for her desire to make the best of a very tough situation.

"It seemed to me that she pretty much accepted the situation for what it was and then made the best of it as she could," Mark said. "She could only type one letter at a time with her mouth but that was OK with her because she was still typing. She tended to look at it: great, I can type rather than it is going to take forever to type a letter but she got pretty fast at it."

Diane's positive attitude helped all of us cope and adjust over the years. We were unique because we were the only couple we knew who both had been stricken by polio. But many other couples were dealing with a spouse who was impacted by the disease. My brother, Jim, recalls hearing that that at least 100 couples got impacted by polio in Denver about the same as we.

"Every one of those couples, except one, got divorced," Jim said. "Grant was the only one who didn't divorce. We all handle things differently... He stuck in there and stayed with Diane and had help."

If Diane had been depressed all the time I'm not sure we could have kept the family together. It was very hard to feel sorry for yourself when Diane had a smile on her face. Her positive attitude also inspired other people.

"She became part of a woman's circle at Park Hill Methodist Church and they would come over to our house," Shari said. "She got to be very close to several women in that organization. The ministers would come to visit her and then they started coming back more often just to sit and talk with her. It was a really stimulating atmosphere."

"People didn't forget her," Mark said. "They didn't forget her because she didn't make it uncomfortable."

Because the children were so close to their mother her death in August 1964 hit them hard. She may have not been able to hug them, dress them or walk them to school but she was always at their side when they were home.

I had taken the boys camping one weekend when Diane fell ill. Shari, getting ready to enter her senior year of high school, was home and called her grandmother. She saw Diane was seriously ill and insisted she go to the hospital even though Diane didn't want to leave home.

"I was home and she just wasn't doing well and I could see it," Shari said. "You prepare all of your life that this is going to happen but wow it was hard. She was only 36."

This was long before cell phones so we didn't know Diane was sick until we returned from camping. She was critical when I got to the hospital and passed away in a few days.

"I remember dad coming to tell us," Shari said. "The call came in the middle of the night. We all kind of sat on the edge of the bed and I remember him crying and you know the three of us were in shock. I was 17, Mark was 14 and Steve was 13."

Her death is still emotional for Mark who choked up when recalling his mother's passing.

"For us, when you have a parent like this, you never felt like you could ever complain about anything in your own life because nothing that was going on could compare (to what she was going through). So, you didn't complain," he said. "What happens is there is a giant hole when she is gone."

"You come home every day and your mom is there," Mark said. "She couldn't take me to the swimming pool but she was always there… I didn't feel allowed to grieve when she died because I was told it really was a blessing. That her suffering was over but I never saw the suffering part of it; I only saw the mom part of it and she was gone. So that was hard."

Mark found Transcendental Meditation (TM) in college. This was way before meditation and yoga were popular in the U.S. and it took me years to really understand it. But I saw the positive change in Mark and that is all that mattered.

"Because I didn't have an outlet to express my grief it internalized itself as anger and there were a few years in there that were pretty tough," Mark said. "I didn't make it easy for anybody else."

Overall, Mark was a good kid but we had our issues. When he was in high school, I expected him to have a short haircut but he let his bangs grow long, which was the style at the time. He refused to cut his hair and went to live with his best friend for something like 72 hours.

Mark said that rebellion came out of the drastic change in his life after his mother's death.

"It was hard and dad had been building a business and traveling a lot and all of a sudden he's sort of had three kids that he maybe didn't know as well as it would have been nice for him. There was a fair amount of conflict and anger," Mark said.

After his mother's death, Mark said he felt like he had no reason to behave.

"We were pretty independent as kids. We were used to a certain routine," he recalled. "I feel like when my mom was there we were really responsible; when we said we were going to be home we were home. But afterwards there was a resistance to restriction. I didn't want anyone telling me what to do. So there was rebellion and anger and it went on for a little while. I feel like I got control of it at maybe 18 or 19. It was into my 20s that I really grieved her death."

Shari also experienced anger after her mother died.

"I was planning to go to college the next year and I said I no longer wanted college. I did not want to go away yet," she said. "They just kept pushing. I remember at Christmas I got so angry and it was my Grandfather Schoelzel who came upstairs. He held me and said I know it is going to be hard but how happy are you living with your dad and your brothers? Maybe going somewhere else will be a nice change for you. I said, OK alright I'll go."

I feel it is important for us to tell our story because most people don't realize the great impact polio has not only on the person afflicted but the family as well. As a family, we were changed by the disease but also enriched by Diane's bravery and positive attitude.

It would take years for us to grieve but her passing also gave me a new lease on life. A pretty woman who grew up on a farm in Nebraska allowed me to have a partner to explore the world and serve Rotary.

Chapter 3

Marlene

My wife and partner for more than 50 years

In my sign business I worked with advertising firms in Denver. At Denver's largest advertising firm in the 1960s – Rippey, Henderson & Bucknum – was a pretty woman from Nebraska who worked in their accounting department. The grocery chain Safeway was one of the firm's clients and we made decals for the Safeway trucks. They also worked with Mountain Bell and we had billboards advertising their Yellow Pages.

While visiting the advertising office one day, I passed by her desk that was near the lobby.

"He said I smiled at him," Marlene recalled. "Well, I smiled at everybody."

That first smile was later followed by a suggestion by Jim Holme, a senior partner in the firm, to ask her out for a drink.

"One day Grant called and asked if I wanted to get a drink after work," Marlene said. "I thought sure why not. To be honest I wasn't sure who was calling. We went to a restaurant downtown and I got a 7-Up or something and we talked for a long time. I thought he was pretty interesting."

I thought she was pretty interesting, too.

Marlene grew up on a small farm in Nebraska where her family raised corn, wheat, cattle, hogs and chickens. Her father came from a long line of farmers. His grandparents came from Germany and farmed and his parents continued the tradition.

My second wife, Marlene Siems, grew up in Nebraska. A family photo taken in 1942 is from left to right: Marlene, 8, her sisters Marjorie, 9 and Judine, 4 and her parents, father, Virgil Siems, 32, and mother, Elisa Siems, 30.

"I'm really glad that I grew up on a farm. I learned a lot," Marlene said. "I think I grew up with a different attitude. The whole family worked even when we were little. Because I was the middle of three girls – I have an older sister and younger sister, and a brother 14 years younger than I am – I got to do the outside work with my dad, which I loved. I worked with farm equipment a lot."

By age 12 when Marlene was tall enough to reach a car clutch she was driving the farm equipment. And that was just her way of life.

"I remember when I was 4 or 5 years old my mom and dad had this big old truck and they would work outside the truck with pitch forks tossing the hay in the truck. It ran in what we called 'grandma gear' so it just crept along. I stood up on the seat to steer but I wasn't supposed to hit anything else and I was kind of scared about that. And if my memory is right my older sister must have been sitting in the other seat holding our baby sister while our parents picked up the hay."

"As we got older we'd milk the cows and feed the chickens and gather the eggs. In those days, families worked together and when needed neighbors helped each other as there was no hired help. The good thing about it is we raised everything we needed to eat," she said.

While Marlene loved the farm, by high school she knew that was not the lifestyle she wanted.

"A lot of kids did not go to college in the area I grew up. I would say about half stayed on the farm. At that point I didn't think I was a farmer and would stay," she said.

She graduated from high school at age 16. In Nebraska, if you attended a junior college you could get a degree to teach in a country school. So, that's what Marlene did. Her one-room schoolhouse had eight students in five different grades. Her oldest student was 13.

All country school teachers were respon- sible for not only pre- paring the curriculum —

Marlene (middle) and her best friends Joan Brolhorst (left) and Engelina Hagemeier attended the one-room Prairie Star School in Nebraska. Marlene and Engelina have remained friends throughout their lives.

Marlene and I often visit Nebraska, and in 2005 we visited the first Homestead Museum near Beatrice, Nebraska.

which included everything from reading and writing to art and music – but also the care and maintenance of the school.

"I taught school one year," Marlene said. "I loved the kids but what I didn't like is that I never felt like I had any spare time. When I went home at night I was always trying to prepare for the next day. I had to clean the school up, light a fire and get the classroom warm. I didn't mind doing all that but it was just mainly preparing the lessons because it took up a lot of time."

But the end of the school year, she knew she didn't want to return and gave notice. She spent that summer helping her father at the farm. Then she got a job in the nearby town of Beatrice working as an accountant at a manufacturing plant that had about 400 employees.

"I worked on a machine that was kind of like the first computer. It was my job to write all the payroll checks at the end of the week. I did it on the machine and I loved that. Everything had to be balanced out and I enjoyed that," she said.

She also made lifelong friends with five of her female colleagues. A few of them took a vacation to Colorado where Marlene's oldest sister, Marj, already had moved and worked first as a secretary in Estes Park for the James family, and later as a teacher in the Denver area.

Marlene dated in Nebraska but stayed single while she watched most of her friends marry. "I had gone to all of their weddings," she recalled. "Back then most girls were getting married right out of high school."

When she was asked why she hadn't married yet, Marlene replied: "My older sister wasn't married either so I'm not going to get married until my older sister gets married and I go to Europe first."

And she stuck to her word. With her sister still single and living in Colorado, Marlene and a friend from work, Iona Hinrichs, quit their jobs in Nebraska and headed to Colorado to find summer work. They ended up working at a shop on top of Trail Ridge Road selling items to tourists.

"There were a couple of park rangers up there, too," Marlene recalled. "We sold some nice Indian jewelry and rugs. We got room and board and a small pay. It was really fun because it was mostly college kids working those summer jobs."

They drove two old station wagons up to Trail Ridge Road every day and stayed at St. Mary's Lodge near town. They got their room and board at the lodge and sometimes were asked to fill in to wait tables or participate in talent shows to entertain the hotel guests.

"I have a special place in my heart for Estes," Marlene said. "Our plan had always been to move to Denver in September and find jobs there, which we did."

In Denver, Marlene, her sister and her friend from Nebraska found an apartment to share near downtown Denver. That's when Marlene started her job at Rippey, Henderson & Bucknum Advertising Agency where we eventually met. She was responsible for billing and payroll.

"I walked just two blocks from our apartment to work," Marlene said. "The best part of my job was that I worked in a high rise building at The Sherman Plaza, and we had the top floor. I got an office that faced directly west. It was so nice that when I got to my desk in the morning I looked outside and saw the mountains! The advertising executives were so creative and very interesting people."

On the weekends, she and her friend would enjoy those mountains whether hiking or skiing. Marlene eventually lost both roommates when her sister, who was teaching in a Denver suburb, got married and moved to Chicago where her husband worked. Her friend from Nebraska moved out when her sister came to Denver and they got a place together.

Marlene lived alone for awhile before her younger sister, Judine, came to Denver and they lived together for about a year. Then she met me.

"By then at work I had moved outside of my beautiful window and inside to a row of desks," Marlene said. "They had changed the office a little bit so I was outside and near the hallway, which I kind of liked because I got to see everybody."

As we got to know each other, I saw she was an independent and adventurous soul. Her first plane ride was with a bunch of women from her office. They rode on a plane round-trip from Lincoln to Omaha, Nebraska just to be able to say they had been on an airplane. As a young adult, she traveled with friends to Europe and took a cruise to Hawaii.

I like to tease her that I saved her from spinsterhood because if a 30-year-old woman wasn't married in those days, people assumed there was something wrong with her. I am eight years older than Marlene but we had a lot of similar interests, especially when it comes to traveling.

48

Marlene didn't worry about being a single woman but felt she was ready to settle down once it was clear we made a good match. Besides, by this time her sister had married and Marlene had been to Europe so she had no more excuses not to settle down.

"Grant and I went skiing and we were riding the ski lift together," my brother, Jim, recalled. "He said to me, 'If I am smart, I am going to marry Marlene.' She is good for him."

About a year after Diane's death I proposed, she said yes and then the next step was telling the children who had already met Marlene and liked her.

"It took Grant a long time to tell the kids we were thinking about getting married," Marlene said. "He must have been nervous because I thought he was going to tell them when they went on a planned trip to California together. So when they came back I asked him if he told them and he said no."

Marlene and I celebrated our wedding on Oct. 23, 1965 and my three children, Steve, 14, Mark, 15 and Shari, 18 welcomed her into the family.

Shari recalls me taking the three kids to dinner and finally telling them our plans to marry. She was attending the University of Northern Colorado and the boys were in high school.

"He said I think your old dad is going to get married," Shari said. "And I said well I don't have an old dad but I guess if this one wants to marry I think that will work. I've always liked her. I think she is a lovely human being. How she puts up with him sometimes, you know how that goes."

Steve, who was a little immature for his age, got excited because he'd have a stepmother who could fix him something new for breakfast each day. Mark liked Marlene but was still dealing with some anger issues.

Mark was mature for his age and often was quiet. He was very responsible when he worked for my sign company as a teenager and never caused any real problems. We didn't know until many years later that he felt like he gave us a hard time when we were first married.

"I'm sure I was hard on her just being a teenager who is angry," Mark recalled. "I'm sure I was not easy during their first few years of marriage. She came into a family with three kids and all of them were a little confused."

Mark echoed those thoughts when he sent Marlene a Mother's Day card after his first son, Ben, was born.

"Mark wrote in the card: Marlene I'm sorry I made your life so difficult the first few years you and Dad were married. He felt really bad," Marlene recalled. "And I told him Mark I don't feel that way at all. He said you are a great grandmother."

Mark and I both recognize that Marlene is a great grandmother and a wonderful great-grandmother the way she takes care of Mark's kids and grandkids.

The one thing Shari noticed immediately after we married is that Marlene was a stickler for getting places on time.

"We all noticed that! My dad was horrible about always being late," Shari said. "Oh Lord! He'd say I'm going to come get you guys at noon and we'll head down to El Paso for spring break. If he got there by 7 p.m. we would not be surprised. Oh, he was really awful because he had nobody to ride herd on him and she whipped him into shape pretty fast around that. We were all surprised when he was on time. It was kind of funny."

Shari, being the oldest child, also appreciated that I needed and wanted the companionship.

"It was nice for him to have someone to go places with," Shari said. "My parents' relationship after they were stricken wouldn't be described as a marriage in many senses of the word because it was not possible. He was on the road so much and he wasn't sitting around and watching TV and talking with her or playing games; it was very different."

I thought Marlene went out of her way to make the boys feel comfortable. She cooked their meals, did their laundry and tried to engage them the best she could. I also thought it was best to move into a new home because their childhood home had so many memories of their mother.

We had to adjust; life went on.

Marlene was aware there would be transitions and some challenges raising two teenage boys. She grew up in a very structured, working family on the farm and had to adjust to city kids who had an unconventional upbringing.

"I always tried to be careful and talk to Grant. I didn't want to be bossy but I was brought up differently than even Grant was. In my family, I saw my folks work so hard that it didn't even occur to me not to help. We certainly didn't think we should be paid for any chores."

One of Steve's chores was to mow the grass. He often was lost in his own world.

"I looked out one day and he made one round (with the mower) and I couldn't see him anywhere," Marlene recalled. "We always ate dinner at the same time, I think it was 6:30 and he was there for dinner. I asked Steve what he had been doing and he said, oh you should go across the road. There was an empty field with all these mice and all these things! That had been where he was all that time instead of mowing. That was Steve."

Marlene adjusted to each child's personality.

"I knew it wasn't easy for them losing their mother,

With three teenagers and our new dog, Duke, we all had adjustments during our first year of marriage in 1966 but Marlene went out of her way to make me and the children happy.

and because I wanted to put Grant first I wanted to do what we had to do to make it work," she said.

Marlene worked for awhile after we were married first full-time at the advertising firm. Then she worked part-time for an association that provided summer camp opportunities for handicapped and mentally challenged children so she could be home when the boys got home from school. But since I was still traveling a lot for work I wanted Marlene to come along and she quit working.

"I loved what we did," Marlene said. "We tried to be together as much as we could. I had a lot of freedom before I was married and now I was ready to enjoy my husband."

We saw many states and many communities those first few years of marriage. My parents would watch the boys and we would head out on a Monday and come home on a Friday.

"We'd go to different towns to "ride the signs" to see if the signs were still standing and in good repair or get leases for new ones," Marlene recalled.

We traveled through many towns in New Mexico and Arizona where our love for Southwestern and Native American art grew. Some of my clients wanted signs along the interstate where the property belonged to the Navajo Nation. I negotiated a deal with the Navajo Tribe so we could put signs on Highway 40 that goes through the Navajo Nation near Grant and Gallup, New Mexico.

During that business trip I met Navajo Roger Davis who ran the Natural Resources Department for the tribe. I had always had an interest in Native Americans but never had a chance to develop a friendship until I met Roger.

We invited Roger and his wife, Florence, and their three children to stay with us when they were traveling to Idaho for a Boy Scout jamboree. We had a large house with several bedrooms so I thought it would be nice for them to stop in Denver on the way. Over the years, our friendship grew and we would visit them in Window Rock, Arizona where Roger was a preacher for a small Presbyterian congregation, after he retired from his job with the Tribe, and the lone member of the choir. His wife played the organ.

We learned a lot about the Navajo Nation. Roger's mother and father were members of the original Council of Navajo Nation. Each time we saw them, they would give us a gift. We have a Navajo wedding basket and two lovely statues decorated with horse hair. Roger passed away but we still keep in touch with Florence and his son, Tony, who later would help a young Chinese student I got to know from the University of Denver.

Our area of travel expanded when a friend and I went in search of buying an island. You read that right, we wanted to buy our own island.

Gene Frink was one of my fraternity brothers at DU. His family owned the Frink Creamery in Denver and they had cheese manufacturing plants in Fort Collins and Larkspur. Gene had visited Hawaii quite a few times as he was growing up because his family had friends there. Around 1966, Gene had seen island land property explode in value and thought the time was ripe to buy an island and make it into the next popular resort.

I was just a newlywed but Marlene said she'd hold down the home front while Gene and I went on an adventure to the South Pacific. We spent

Marlene and I traveled throughout the Southwest and got to know Navajos Roger and Florence Davis of Window Rock, Arizona. On their way to a Scout Jamboree in 1967 they traveled with their children – Snookie, Gummy, Duddy - and a girl cousin through Denver and stayed at our home.

about two weeks visiting Fiji, Tahiti, New Zealand and Australia looking for a good investment.

I think Mark turned 18 while I was gone and Marlene was concerned about whether there would be any problems when he was celebrating his 18th birthday. But it worked out fine while I was gone.

Gene and I stayed with friends in Australia and mostly saw the Sydney area. In New Zealand, we basically stayed in the Auckland area but did drive around the northern island. We didn't have much luck in Fiji either and came back without seeing anything we liked.

Then the Wall Street Journal had a story about a Canadian man who was looking for partners to buy an island in Fiji that was owned by a New Zealander. It was named Wakaya and located in the heart of the Fiji archipelago, just 14 miles from Levuka, the first capitol of the Fiji islands.

Gene and I signed up along with Boulder resident Lou Gragg, who was the owner of competitive sign business but also a friend. We became owners of the island along with the Canadian investor and five other investors from Seattle. The island was five miles long with 21 beautiful, white sandy beaches, coral reefs and an old plantation house. The island's primary crop was coconuts but it also had wild boars, wild turkeys and wild deer on it.

Marlene was supportive when we bought the island because it wasn't a huge investment by today's standard and she was looking forward to another adventure.

We typically visited once a year with Gene and his wife or Lou and his wife. If we weren't on the beach, we'd hike the Milford Track in New Zealand or visit Australia. We were in that ownership for several years before we got an offer from a British development company. Interestingly enough, that same British corporation ended up owning the Denver Tech Center, just a few miles from our home in Denver.

I and eight others owned an island named Wakaya and located in the heart of the Fiji archipelago, just 14 miles from Levuka, the first capitol of the Fiji islands. We have wonderful memories of vacationing there.

Wakaya is now a $1,200-a-day resort. I don't know whether people have built private homes there or they built a lodge. I'm not sorry we sold it when we did because we made money on it and we had fun when we had it. We and the other two Colorado couples who had invested in Wakaya took that money and bought a 160-acre plantation on one of the big islands in Fiji called Vanua Levu. Fiji has 300 islands but the one with our plantation was one of the largest at 100 miles long.

We had a house there but it wasn't too swift so we usually stayed at a hotel a few miles down the road. All three couples enjoyed that plantation for 25 years. One year, Marlene and I hosted our entire family on a vacation there. I remember that clearly because Mark's oldest son, Ben, was a newborn and the Fijians, who were wonderful people, were in awe of the small white baby. Many asked to hold him and Ben just fit in the palm of their hand. My parents and aunt also came on that trip and we have grand memories of Fiji.

We ended up selling that plantation to some people from Hollywood.

Among the other highlights of our traveling adventures have been photographing African wildlife on a safari, floating the Grand Canyon, snowshoeing among the geysers, buffalo and elk in Yellowstone National Park and climbing a 14,000-foot peak in Colorado on my 50th birthday.

So, we were world travelers before and after I joined the Rotary Club of Denver in 1969. Our view of the world expanded even more when I was elected District Governor 5450 in 1984-85, which led to expanding my work with Rotary International and more adventures worldwide.

Marlene was always supportive with my Rotary work and I am grateful I was by her side when she suffered a great tragedy in 1971.

Both of her parents died in a car accident. They had driven to Beatrice, Nebraska to bring both of their mothers fresh eggs from their farm and visit. Marlene's grandmothers were still living in their own homes there.

"My parents were on their way home on a paved road that was two lanes," Marlene recalled. "They were just driving along when a lady driving a car came towards them. There may have been a place she drove off the edge of the road and when she overcorrected she crashed right into them. They died instantly. The lady was thrown out of her car. I didn't know her and she survived."

"It was hard for everyone, especially my grandmothers. In fact, that happened on Dec. 16 and I can remember because both of my grandmothers were pretty healthy and my sisters and I went home to take care of the funeral arrangements. My Grandmother Lancaster, my mom's mother, kept saying we had to eat. Then Christmas day or the day before Christmas she got sick and went to the hospital and she died. I said she died of a broken heart."

We can never know from day to day what challenges life will bring us. I guess that's one reason I feel so passionate about trying to make a difference through my work with Rotary. The Rotary Club of Denver led to many other opportunities with Rotary International, which Marlene and I experienced together.

Anyone who has worked with a community service or non-profit organization knows how important it is to have a supportive spouse. I hit the jackpot with Marlene.

Chapter 4

The Rotary Club of Denver

My touchstone for Rotary

By 1969, Marlene and I were empty nesters with the kids moving on with their lives. I also was facing an early retirement from the sign business because of Lady Bird Johnson, President Lyndon Johnson's wife.

When President Johnson assumed office his wife decided it was time to get rid of all the highway advertising signs cluttering our interstate highways, which now would be called eye pollution. She urged Congress to pass the Highway Beautification Act of 1965.

There were two kinds of highway advertising signs. For my business, 90 percent of our signs were permanent signs for the top oil companies: Chevron, Conoco, Exxon and Phillips. These signs had reflective tape baked into the enamel signs that reflected off motor vehicle headlights in the dark. The signs directed motorists to the nearest gas stations. Our signs were different from billboards, which were paper and about every month different companies were advertised with new paper covering the old paper.

At the height of our business, we had 1,800 signs in 13 Western states. We had always worked hard to keep our signs maintained but admittedly some other companies did not, and in parts of the country landowners crammed numerous signs on small plots of land.

Suddenly, the federal government had this new law and had no idea how to fairly compensate the sign businesses for the loss of advertising revenue. It became a long, drawn-out process and I made many trips to Washington, D.C., to discuss the issue with the Federal Highway Administration (FHA).

My father, Clarence, and I started Mountain States Advertising. We purchased signs from Western Goodroads that they had in Colorado, Wyoming and New Mexico. Then we expanded to build our own double-faced signs for Mountain States Telephone Yellow Pages placed in the states of Colorado, Wyoming, New Mexico, Arizona, Utah, Montana, Idaho, North Dakota, South Dakota, Nebraska, Kansas and Oklahoma.

The FHA had no history in this area and I recommended they hire Jack Francis who worked for the Utah Highway Department. Jack had become an expert in buying and condemning signs in Utah as new development took place in the state. He understood how the process could work successfully and I thought he would help the federal government implement the new law.

The FHA leadership took my advice, hired Jack and he worked for several years with the FHA to develop a fair plan. Jack was a tremendous help to the sign company owners but we also still had to work with the FHA and Congress.

I often traveled to meetings also attended by Doug Snarr who was the owner of Snarr Advertising in Utah. We were two of the largest sign owners in the country. Once the FHA had a plan, then I had to work with my clients who had leased signs in 13 states. In Colorado, I worked with Charlie Shumate, who was head of the Colorado Department of Highways at the time, and Al Vonderheid, who was the sign appraiser for CDOT.

John Volpe was the U.S. Secretary of Transportation when the Highway Beautification Act was passed and he worked with all of the sign companies. To ceremoniously kick off the Highway Beautification Act, Volpe flew to Denver and we met him at Stapleton International Airport. We then drove him to one of the signs my business owned along Interstate 70 east of Aurora and Volpe took a chain saw to the sign and ceremoniously cut it down. We took a home movie of the ceremony and local newspapers wrote about it. Why did Volpe have the ceremony in Denver? I can't remember if we talked him into it, if he wanted to come to Denver or if he already was going to be in Denver for something else. It was kind of fun that the first sign to be cut down was mine.

Jack Francis recalled that in four years, 700,000 highway advertising signs were removed.

In the middle of all my work wrapping up the highway advertising sign business, I decided it was time to join the Rotary Club of Denver in 1969. I was only 43 so I knew I wanted something worthwhile to keep me busy in my forced early retirement once all the issues with the FDA and sign holders were resolved.

Look what happens when you call Long Distance.
Pick up your phone and go visiting tonight!

MOUNTAIN STATES TELEPHONE (A) *It's fast and easy to Dial Direct!*

Part of our business was running advertisements for Mountain States Telephone, which were done at Rippey, Henderson & Bucknum Advertising where Marlene worked and where we met.

I didn't need to find a new career because I had enough money with the sign compensations that if I was cautious and invested wisely, Marlene and I would have a comfortable retirement. We wouldn't be wealthy but we could get along.

That early retirement allowed me to focus my energy into Rotary. There were so many good projects underway locally and worldwide and I was very excited to dive in. Marlene was supportive of my Rotary work from Day One.

"Well, it didn't surprise me he wanted to join," Marlene said. "I knew about Rotary because when I worked at the ad agency several of our men joined. I kind of learned about it and I wrote the Rotary dues checks for those men. When I met Grant he talked about his dad being a Rotarian."

The first few years I focused on the local projects that Denver Rotarians had developed. I chaired the Denver Kids committee for one year. The Denver Public Schools started the program to match underprivileged students with mentors. They had so many children in need that they turned to Rotary and asked the club to get involved. There are about 1,100 students in the program now. The Rotarian mentors meet with the students and encourage them to do well in school. Some mentors also take their students on extra-curricular activities, such as day trips or to professional sporting events or plays.

Marlene and I sponsored a young boy, David Sarno, who was being raised by a single mother. His father had left them when David was a baby. He lived with his mom and aunt who did the best they could. We just added a little encouragement for him to do well in school and stay out of trouble as he grew into a teenager and young adult.

One goal of the program is to introduce the kids to activities outside of their normal routines. We took David fishing up to Elk Falls Ranch in the mountains outside of Denver. One time we took him on a back-packing trip to Durango in southwest Colorado. We rode horses 10

Among the many great programs Denver Rotary sponsors is Denver Kids, which matches underprivileged children with Rotary members as mentors. Marlene and I became friends with David Sarno and in 1973 we took him camping in the Weminuche Wilderness near Creede, Colorado. David has grown into a lovely man with his own family.

miles up a mountain trail and they dropped us off at the camp. We fished and saw wildlife.

David turned out to be a nice man who never smoked or drank. We still keep in touch with him, his wife and their children.

But not all Denver Kids partnerships have a happy ending. My brother, Jim, had joined Rotary and at one time he, our father and I were all members together. Jim had been a successful salesman with a major paper company and worked out of Denver. When his company wanted to transfer him out of state, his wife and children did not want to leave Denver and Jim started a second successful career in real estate.

Jim became a mentor in the Denver Kids program.

"It is a great program with many success stories. I've been involved with it for years," Jim recalled. "But my experience with mentoring was not successful. I told them to give me the toughest kid they had and they did."

Jim was paired with a 16-year-old Native American teenager who said he was the great grandson of Sitting Bull. His father was an alcoholic and his mother was in prison for killing a woman by slitting her throat. The boy was in a foster home with about 12 other children and had major issues. Jim tried to help him get on a better path but the teenager resisted any help.

"He ended up in jail twice and probably is in prison today," Jim said. "I tried and it just didn't work out. If you get to the kids when they are younger and a little more stable we can make a difference. We've had some amazing success stories but mine wasn't one of them."

Still, Jim didn't get discouraged and continues to work with Denver Kids and other programs. The key is this kind of community service does make a difference in individual's lives and the community, and we didn't get discouraged when things didn't work out well.

In 1978, I was elected as president of Club 31. The Rotary Club of Denver at the time had 625 members and was one of the largest clubs in the world. It was quite an honor my peers bestowed on me and I took the job seriously. The term is only for one year but I did my best to build up membership and keep our programs moving forward.

Rotary didn't allow women members until 1989 but the members' wives were active in social events and often behind the scenes by supporting their husbands.

"It was really easy for me to get involved because they had women groups," Marlene said. "We didn't meet that often but we had events like visiting the Capitol building. We also had a small fundraiser for our nurses' scholarship fund. It was a good way to get acquainted. For dinner we had social events with Rotary and we all attended because we had become friends."

In 1980, the Denver Rotary Club Foundation set an ambitious goal to raise $1 million by the club's 75th anniversary in 1986. Marlene and I had gotten into the early phase of art collection and had attended national shows, including the Cowboy Artists of America in Phoenix and the Prix de West in Oklahoma City. We met some of the leading artists in the country at the shows.

One of our most prized sculptures, called Pueblo Woman, was created by Allan Houser of Santa Fe who became our friend. The Smithsonian Museum of the American Indian borrowed this sculpture from us for its opening in 2004 and kept it for one and a half years.

One of our most prized sculptures, called Pueblo Woman, was created by Allan Houser of Santa Fe who became our friend. The Smithsonian Museum of the American Indian borrowed this sculpture from us for its opening in 2004 and kept it for one and a half years.

Houser was head of the sculpture department at the Institute of American Indian Arts in Santa Fe until 1975 when he started focusing on his own work. He created a large body of sculptures in bronze, stone and wood, which are popular worldwide. In 1992, he received The National Medal of Arts, America's highest arts award, from President George H. W. Bush.

Houser died in 1994 but his art lives on at many museums and galleries worldwide and at the presidential libraries of George H. W. Bush and Bill Clinton.

My interest and knowledge in Native American art expanded through my work as a board member at Millicent Rogers Museum in Taos, New Mexico, which is dedicated to "sharing and celebrating the arts and cultures of the Southwest."

In 1947, Millicent Rogers, a granddaughter of one of the original founders of Standard Oil and a talented designer and patron of the arts, moved to Taos. She had an extensive collection of Native American jewelry and weavings. Millicent died of an enlarged heart in 1952 when she was only 50, and a museum was opened in her honor at a temporary location.

In 1968, the museum moved to its permanent site, which was a ranch home built by Claude J.K. and Elizabeth Anderson. In the 1980s, the home was renovated and expanded by noted architect Nathaniel A. Owings, a fellow member of the Millicent Rogers board. Over the years, the museum acquired a large collection of Zuni and Hopi kachina figures and Indian pottery dating back to 1400s. It also features Hispanic artists, Santos religion icons and ancient weavings. The museum is located four miles north of Taos Plaza on a high ridge amidst sagebrush and sage. Many people have commented that it is the best museum that celebrates Southwest art and culture, especially because it has the Maria Martinez family collection of her world famous pottery from the San Ildefonso Pueblo.

I served on the museum board with former Taos Pueblo governor Tony Reyna.

Tony is a very interesting guy. He was born in Taos Pueblo in 1916 and built a home that also served as an art shop when as he said banks "weren't lending money to Indians." After serving in World War II and surviving the horrific 65-mile Bataan Death March in the Philippines, he opened Tony Reyna's Indian Shop, which has attracted people throughout the world, including former President Jimmy Carter and Princess Anne of Great Britain.

While my interest in Native American art grew as an adult, the roots really were planted when I was a child. We used to have family vacations in Pecos, New Mexico and I would search for and collect arrow heads I found there, which was on land that is now the Pecos National Monument. That probably is one reason I also was intrigued with Mesa Verde National Park in southwest Colorado.

Mesa Verde near Cortez is very unique because of the preserved ruins that tourists can walk through. The Anasazi Indians lived in the dwellings carved into a mountain. It almost looks like an ancient apartment building. They abruptly abandoned the site and hundreds of years later the U.S. government smartly made it a national park after many artifacts were found there.

Marlene and I enjoyed visiting Mesa Verde and I joined the Board of Directors where I served for the 10-year limit and then my brother, Jim, replaced me. In 2016, Jim serves as chairman of the board and works very hard at that position.

I worked on several projects to improve and preserve the park. Mesa Verde is tucked among land off the interstate highway and during my time on the board we wanted to give it more exposure. We helped get a $12.1 million visitor center built at the entrance to the park, which is designated one of 20 "World Heritage Sites" in the U.S.

Marlene and I gained more knowledge of southwestern art while staying at our townhome in Santa Fe and visiting Taos, New Mexico. Our Denver Rotary Club president Preston Smith and his wife, Carolyn, visited an art show while in California and we began discussing an art show sponsored by Denver Rotary to raise money for the foundation.

I proposed an annual art show in Denver called "Artists of America" that would not only raise money for the Denver Rotary Foundation but

I served a 10-year term on the Mesa Verde National Park Board of Directors and helped get a $12.1 million visitor center built at the entrance to the park, which is designated one of 20 "World Heritage Sites" in the U.S.

also the Colorado History Museum, which would display the art for six weeks each fall.

"Grant had lots of contacts that would be critical to the future of Artists of America," Carolyn Smith told author Rosemary Fetter in the Rotary's 100th anniversary book.

Governor Richard Lamm, who was an honorary member of our club, backed the idea of the art show not only to benefit our foundation but also to promote Denver in the art world and help the local economy.

We tried to lure an art show from Oklahoma City to Denver but that fell apart. Then we convened a meeting in Santa Fe with top artists including

Glenna Goodacre, Wilson Hurley, Bettina Steinke, Clark Hulings and Everett Raymond Kintsler.

We told the artists we wanted a show better than the ones in Phoenix and Oklahoma City and welcomed their suggestions on how to make that happen. They suggested we open the show to established American artists and not just Western artists, and do away with the juried part of other shows.

Our first show on September 11, 1981 took place at the Colorado Heritage Center, which later became the Colorado History Museum. The artists kept about 70 to 75 percent of the profit from the sales, with the remaining profits split among the Denver Rotary Foundation and the Colorado History Museum.

We had a preview exhibition and sale and then the artwork was displayed for the public at the museum for six weeks. We had 150 volunteers, including Rotary wives who were trained to be docents and tell visitors about the art. Sixty-six artists displayed 159 paintings and more than 1,000 guests bid on and bought the works of art.

That first year, we gave billionaire businessman Phil Anschutz a private viewing because he was just starting to amass one of the largest western

In 1990, artist Daniel Greene did a portrait demonstration of me as part of the Artists of America yearly fundraiser for the Rotary Club of Denver.

art collections in the world. A lot of people doubted we could make this art show a success but after the first night we had sold nearly $1 million worth of art.

Over its 20-year history, Artists of America generated $14 million in art sales with $1.9 million going to the Denver Rotary Foundation and $804,000 to the Colorado History Museum. The foundation used that money to support numerous youth-oriented programs and educational opportunities in our city and state.

The public also enjoyed the shows and the history museum bussed in school children from across the state to see the exhibits each year.

Artists of America became the favorite art show of many notable artists. I had been chairman of the program for five years and then passed that baton off to others. My brother, Jim, also volunteered as a salesman each year.

In 1990, Denver Rotary's Artists of America video won the Rocky Mountain Regional Emmy in the non-news academy. The film also was recognized by the New York and Houston film festivals and U.S. Industrial Film Festivals.

Each year the art show raised money but after the event in 2001, a few of our Rotarians decided to end the project, which was something I learned about after the decision was made. I believe if the issue had been put to a vote to our entire membership the art show would have continued. But sometimes you just have to accept a decision and move on.

Besides, by this time my brother, Jim, had started another fundraiser for the foundation. Jim had heard about the Houston Rotary's Lombardi Award, which was named after the legendary NFL coach Vince Lombardi and helped raise money for the Houston Rotary through a yearly banquet. Proceeds went to a Houston hospital that treated children with cancer.

Denver had finally been awarded a Major League Baseball team in 1993, which was called the Colorado Rockies.

Modeling a fundraiser after the Houston program, Jim decided to give an award to a MLB player each year based on that player's community service. He named the award after Branch Rickey, a MLB team owner who helped break the color barrier when he welcomed Jackie Robinson to the Brooklyn Dodgers in 1947.

"Rickey made a number of contributions to the game, but more important, he was a great humanitarian who exemplifies what Rotary stands for – 'Service Above Self,' " Jim said. The first Branch Rickey Award was presented in 1992 to Dave Winfield of the Toronto Blue Jays. The banquet,

My brother, Jim, started the Branch Rickey Award as another fundraiser for Denver Rotary. I helped get artist George Lundeen to create a 13-foot bronze sculpture called The Player (pictured here in clay in his studio) which stands on a four-foot granite base at the main entrance of Coors Field. A plaque displays the names of the Branch Rickey Award winners and donors who made the sculpture possible

co-sponsored by Rotary and the Colorado Rockies Foundation, attracted more than 500 people. It became a major fundraiser for our club for 23 years, and my brother, Jim, should get credit for creating the award.

In 2005, I chaired Denver Rotary Club's Centennial project for Rotary International's 100th birthday. Each club worldwide was asked to do something to recognize Rotary's milestone. I thought a great way to do that was to highlight our Branch Rickey award. My brother, Jim, had wanted to get a statue in front of Coors Field, home of the Colorado Rockies, commemorating the Branch Rickey Award for several years but ran into some hassles at city hall. I made some calls, including engaging artist George Lundeen and getting a $25,000 donation from team owners Dick and Charlie Monfort.

Rotarian John Hickenlooper, who was mayor at the time, helped clear up issues with the city.

Lundeen created a 13-foot sculpture called The Player, which stands on a four-foot granite base at the main entrance of Coors Field. A plaque displays the names of the Branch Rickey Award winners.

The statue was dedicated on June 2, 2005. Former Denver Mayor Wellington Webb, who was Denver's first African-American mayor and a Rotarian, attended the ceremony. He recalled growing up on the south side of Chicago as a White Sox fan and his memories of seeing Jackie Robinson play the Chicago Cubs during one of his rare trips to Wrigley Field with his father. He said he and his father "admired Branch Rickey for having the guts" to change sports history and as a result helped lead to changes elsewhere in society.

Also at the ceremony were Rickey's grandson, who thanked Rotary for recognizing his grandfather, and the Rockies owners, who said the team sought players with the character that Branch Rickey would seek out.

The statue has been seen by millions of people who have passed by it, including baseball fans who attended the Colorado Rockies first appearance in the World Series in 2007. My hope is that when people see that statue and read the inscriptions they will understand the good work Rotary does worldwide.

The Branch Rickey Award ended after 23 years when MLB lost interest in nominating players but that project raised a lot of money for our community projects. The statue outside of Coors Field will always be a testament to the good that project did.

In addition to raising money for our local Rotary projects, all local Rotary clubs donate money to the Rotary International Foundation, which funds projects around the world. The foundation began in 1917 with a donation of $26.50 from the Rotary Club of Kansas City, Missouri. Rotary President Arch Klumph proposed the endowment "for the purpose of doing good in world."

By 1930, the Foundation awarded its first grant, $500 to the International Society for Crippled Children later renamed Easter Seals.

When I was chosen as Governor of Rotary District 545 (now District 5450) in 1984-1985, I wanted to focus on increasing the amount each Rotarian in my district contributed to the Rotary International Foundation. At that time, the District 5450 boundaries included 65 clubs in northern Colorado, Wyoming and Nebraska.

I thought one way to raise more money was to encourage more of our members to be Paul Harris Fellows. The recognition was named after Rotary's founder and was given to each Rotarian who donated at least $1,000 to the Foundation. Some people gave $100 a year and after 10 years they automatically become a Paul Harris Fellow. In the old days it was very common for members to spread out the donations but some gave $1,000 in one shot because they didn't want to wait to become a Paul Harris Fellow.

But when I joined Denver Rotary in 1969 I don't think we had a half dozen people in our whole club of more than 600 members who were Paul Harris Fellows. It just wasn't a popular thing to do and it wasn't publicized. The Rotarians didn't fully understand how the donations were being put to good use worldwide.

The Rotary theme my year as district governor was "Discover A New World of Service," and it was part of our World President Carlos Canseco's

In 1984, while serving as a Rotary International District Governor, I traveled to Boca Raton, Florida for a convention also attended by Rotary International President Carlos Canseco, who began the PolioPlus program.

theme of promoting Rotary projects worldwide. I had lapel pins made for about $1 a piece with that theme. I gave each Rotarian who donated at least $100 to Rotary International a pin and I also promised each club president who got 100 percent of his members to give at least $100 that he could sit with me at the head table during our district convention, which that year was held in the prestigious Broadmoor Hotel in Colorado Springs.

Marlene and I packed up the car and hit the road with the goal to visit all 65 clubs and we did. That brought us to cities and small rural towns. This was a time when Rotary still didn't allow female members but Marlene was greeted by the wives and entertained while I met with local Rotary leaders and spoke at their membership meetings.

"Grant would leave about 10 a.m. to meet with the officers of the club and I would usually meet with the wives for lunch," Marlene recalled. "Or sometimes the women would want to show me something in the town. I remember one gal and she was so cute. She had a brand new baby and grandma lived with her. She wanted me to see their new history museum. She picked me up at 11 a.m. and then we had to stop by her house so that she would nurse the baby."

We share one funny story that shows the dynamics of Rotary because no two clubs are the same.

We went to a mid-size town in Wyoming and the president of the club told Marlene to meet us at a local hotel for lunch with his wife and other wives of club members. While I visited with the club president and membership, Marlene arrived at the hotel and waited in the lobby.

And she waited and waited.

"I saw some women bringing in gifts and I asked them if they were Rotarian wives but they said no, they were having a baby shower," Marlene said. "So I continued to wait in the lobby until I saw the club president with Grant and I went over to him and said I hadn't seen the ladies yet."

It turns out the women had come in from another entrance. The club president directed Marlene to the room that had several people eating lunch, including the Rotarian wives.

"There was a table with eight places and one empty for me. The women were all talking among themselves already and I thought oh well and I'll just observe," Marlene said. "Pretty soon a woman at a separate table poked the president's wife and asked, 'Is this your bridge group?' She said, "No, it's that once-a-year Rotary nonsense.'"

I laughed when Marlene told me the story and thought my speech to encourage the members to become Paul Harris Fellows likely fell flat. We both were shocked when a week later I got a note and check from the club. They borrowed money out of their treasury to send $100 each for every one of their members. So, it was clear they listened and realized the importance of Rotary International's projects.

The other response throughout the district was positive and during my year as district governor we raised more than $500,000 for the Rotary International Foundation, and we were the Number 1 district in fundraising among Rotary's world of 500 or so districts. This included the first ever Rotary International scholarship in perpetuity for $150,000 given by my fellow Denver Rotarian Temple Hoyne Buell, who was Denver's premier architect. That caught the eye of the Rotary International leadership in Evanston, Illinois. They wondered what was up with this district governor in Colorado. After my term ended, I was appointed to the Rotary International Finance Committee, which I chaired for one year.

In 1993-95, my two-year term as Rotary International Director was fun because it was the first time the other U.S. Directors (there are 18 Directors worldwide) in my region weren't from California, Michigan or Illinois. I was the first Director for my zone from Colorado in many years. The other closest Directors were in Kansas City and Omaha. We jokingly called ourselves "The Midwest Mafia." Because we were all situated in the same part of the country, we and our spouses got to know each other very well and worked well together.

I also thought it would be a good idea for Rotary's World President to visit Denver once a year after his visit to the annual Rose Bowl Parade in Pasadena, California. Rotary always has a float in the parade and sometimes the president rides on it or just attends the festivities. The Rotary club in Pasadena has a reception or function for their club members to get to know the president.

I thought it would be great to have the World President stop in Denver on his way back to his housing at Rotary headquarters in Evanston. The first president I invited was Carlos Canseco from Monterey, Mexico. It began a tradition that has lasted more than 30 years. The World President stops in Denver for a president's dinner with Denver area Rotarians and a fundraising event for Rotary International.

"The World President stops in Denver because of Grant," Rotarian John Klug said. "Grant knows so many people and he is highly respected."

When Jim Lacy was World President he also attended a conference of Rotarians from Loveland, Greeley and Fort Collins in Estes Park. I told Jim to expect to see a lot of elk when we got to Estes. Of course that was the one day the elk were hiding. We laugh about that and I send him photographs of the elk Marlene and I see when we visit Estes.

At the same time I was district governor, Rotary International was planning to do what it had never done before: have one corporate worldwide project where all clubs would participate. Previously, individual clubs had projects in all parts of the world but Rotary International never had called on all Rotarians to ban together for one cause.

Little did I know that more than 30 years after polio changed my life, Rotary International would be a driving force to eradicate the disease worldwide.

Chapter 5

PolioPlus

My role in eradicating polio worldwide

M ost younger generations of Americans have never heard of polio, which is good and bad. Good because it shows we have successfully eradicated the disease from our country but bad because there is still a threat the disease could raise its ugly head without proper immunization.

So, let me give you a little history about the disease.

Polio dates back to ancient times when Egyptians contracted the paralyzing and deadly disease. The first cluster of outbreaks in the United States was reported in the late 1800s in New York, Louisiana and Boston. In 1894, the first reported epidemic in the U.S. hit Vermont where 132 people were infected and 18 people died. In the early 1900s, several cities were hit by waves of polio patients, including 2,500 people in New York City.

The patient load grew so large for some hospitals that they had to create polio isolation wards in gymnasiums.

By 1952, a reported 58,000 Americans had been afflicted with polio with 3,145 deaths. Another 21,000 lost the use of their limbs. The number of cases dropped dramatically in 1955 when Jonas Salk discovered the first polio vaccination, followed by Albert Sabin's oral vaccination in 1961. There is no cure so vaccination is the best way to protect people and it is the only way to stop the disease from spreading. By 1979, polio was eradicated in the U.S. but it was still killing and paralyzing children and adults worldwide.

Reports showed that in 1985 there were more than 125 countries where polio still was an epidemic and 350,000 children infected worldwide.

In 1978, Rotary International started a Health, Hunger and Humanity Program (3-H) to focus on issues worldwide. A year later, the President of Rotary International, James Bomar Jr. from Tennessee, suggested a major immunization campaign in the Philippines because in his travels he saw many children crawling on their hands and knees who had been afflicted by polio. He discovered most of the children had never received the polio vaccination.

With the help of Rotarians in the Philippines, the 3-H committee and hundreds of volunteers, more than six million children age 5 and under were immunized in 1979.

Once Rotarians in other countries heard about the immunization day, they began organizing similar events in their countries.

Our World President Carlos Canseco at the time was a medical doctor and he proposed Rotary take on the eradication of polio worldwide as a corporate project. The next step was to create an advisory committee and my name was proposed because many of my Rotarian friends knew my history with the disease.

Our campaign to raise $120 million for PolioPlus started in 1986 and at the Rotary Convention in Philadelphia in 1988 we celebrated raising $244 million to help eradicate polio worldwide.

This was the first time in Rotary history that they ever hired a professional fundraiser. It was a firm out of New York who advised Rotary how to go about raising the goal of $120 million to immunize 500 million children worldwide. Once a plan was in place, Rotarians were chosen to oversee the fundraising and work out of headquarters in Illinois.

We knew that Rotarians in poor countries like India could not raise a lot of money but every Rotarian in the world was asked to participate in the cause.

My role was to give speeches to Rotarians to tell them my story with polio and educate them about how the disease still affected children and adults worldwide. It was very important to do the speeches because polio had been eradicated in the U.S. and many Rotarians did not understand that the disease still impacted many countries.

I took great pride in the fact that the Rotary Club of Denver raised more than $526,902 for PolioPlus by 1988 – the highest amount raised by any individual Rotary club in the world. A big factor in our success was that in addition to me, several members of our club had polio as children or in their families and understood the impact of the disease. Club member Dick Reuss was the campaign leader and the Colorado Trust awarded our club a $100,000 challenge grant.

Our club President Dave Fleming gave the vaccine to his grandson at one of our club meetings.

Rotarians worldwide shocked a lot of people when we surpassed the $120 million goal and hit about $247 million in three years. Still, we were naïve to think even that amount would eradicate polio. Originally, the program was called PolioPlus because we planned to first vaccinate the children for polio and then five other common diseases. Well, we soon discovered that wasn't going to work because of the cost. It cost about 12 cents to give a child two drops by mouth of the polio vaccine but other immunizations required needles and more money.

We soon decided we better stick to polio alone and just be thankful to get it done.

"I don't think anyone at that time really imagined how much money and how much time and effort it would really take to do this job," recalled Jim Lacy, who has chaired the original advisory committee since its inception, and served as Rotary International President from 1998-99.

Our efforts attracted the attention of the World Health Organization, which became our partner along with the U.S. Centers for Disease Prevention, Centers for Disease Control and Prevention (CDC) and UNICEF.

Jim Lacy also became the national director for the PolioPlus campaign. He had a great business background having run the Gilliam Candy Brands for years and remains as chairman of the board for the company. They manufacture candy in plants in Kentucky, New York, Kansas and Georgia.

His son, Bill, worked for President Ronald Reagan and knew Senate Majority Leader Bob Dole. Bill urged his father to ask Congress to provide funding for PolioPlus. Jim understood how government worked having served two terms as a state representative in the Tennessee General Assembly.

Jim and Les Wright, also a member of the PolioPlus committee, went to Washington, D.C. and met with Dole. Dole was so impressed with their presentation that he contacted USAID, the agency that oversees global poverty projects, and suggested they find funding for our project. Jim and Les had to return to Washington, D.C., about three weeks later and gave their presentation again.

After that meeting, USAID contributed about $10 million annually to the cause. Our committee members have traveled to D.C. every year since to thank Congress for the funding and remind them the job is not yet done. Jim also spent many years alone visiting D.C. and lobbying members of Congress to keep the funding and for years he called each Congress member to make sure we had their support. Rotary International eventually hired a full-time lobbyist but Jim is still involved.

"Congress is always amazed how much Rotarians do and how much money Rotarians have raised," Lacy said.

Congress allocated $214 million in 2016 toward the polio eradication effort worldwide, and nearly $2 billion total over the years. By 2016, Rotary International had raised $9.5 billion to eradicate polio worldwide. An estimated $1.5 billion will still be needed to immunize children worldwide until about 2020 to make sure the disease is truly eradicated.

While that is an outstanding amount of money to fight the disease, studies show that more than $50 billion is actually saved in the next 20 years because that would be the cost of helping children and adults paralyzed by the disease.

Other countries also have recognized the importance of eradicating polio and by 2016 more than $19 billion from other countries also has been raised to fight the disease.

While raising money is important, ongoing education also is an important part of the cause. I used my connections with artist Glenna Goodacre in 1986 and approached her about creating small bronze statutes to help with fundraising efforts.

"My own children were immunized years ago," Goodacre told the Rotarian Magazine. "So when Grant first told me about polio still being a problem in the world, I was just amazed. I wanted to do my part to help. I visualized a man administering vaccine to a baby while sitting on a crate in a field, which could be anywhere in the world. At his knee are two older children of different ethnic backgrounds."

She made several different sizes of the bronze statues that could rest on a desk or table and members received one based on their donation. For example, if you gave $10,000 to $50,000 you got a small version and a larger one if a donation was $100,000.

By 1991, Rotary leaders asked Goodacre to create a larger-than-life replica of the statue to display in front of Rotary World Headquarters in Evanston, Illinois. Goodacre had lived in Colorado for 10 years and had her work done at one of the best foundries in the world located in Loveland, Colorado and owned by Richard Gooding, the former owner of a Pepsi-Cola plant in Denver and a member of the Rotary Club of Denver.

Gooding donated the cost to cast the statue and he thought it was only fitting to have another larger-than-life statue in Denver.

In 1995, more than 400 people gathered in Denver for the dedication of one of the large statues in downtown Denver. The statue includes a plaque that reads that PolioPlus is "Rotary's Gift to the Children of the World."

"I am proud to be here as a fellow Rotarian because I know this represents the kind of good work we do," said Denver Mayor Wellington Webb, a member of the Denver Rotary Club, at the ceremony.

The Denver statue was later moved to the University of Colorado Anschutz Medical Campus in nearby Aurora, Colorado, which also houses Children's Hospital. The Boettcher Foundation gave a grant of $14,200 to relocate the statue there. It is used as an educational tool for C.U.'s medical, dental and nursing schools at the campus.

In 1995, more than 400 people gathered in Denver for the dedication of one of the large statues in downtown Denver created by artist Glenna Goodacre for polio awareness. The statue includes a plaque that reads that PolioPlus is "Rotary's Gift to the Children of the World." It was later moved to the University of Colorado Anschutz Medical Campus in nearby Aurora, Colorado, which also houses Children's Hospital.

Two other replicas of the statue are at Children's Hospital in Omaha and in Cincinnati, Ohio.

Another inspirational moment for me and Marlene is when we represented Rotary at a National Immunization Day in the Ivory Coast of Africa in 1998. Rotarians in the Ivory Coast worked with Rotary volunteers from around the world to organize the event, educate local parents and help place the two drops of polio vaccine in children's mouths age 5 and under.

Marlene and I traveled with Elizabeth "Betty" Bumpers (the wife of U.S. Senator Dale Bumpers), the Minister of Health of the Ivory Coast, who was a graduate of a U.S. medical school, and representatives of the CDC and WHO. At our first stop we gave

Marlene and I have traveled to several National Immunization Days worldwide to provide the polio vaccination to children.

ceremonial speeches before the immunizations began and my speech was to represent Rotary International.

That day was the hottest day I had ever endured. It must have been 98 degrees with 98 percent humidity. I had a coat and tie on because the Minister of Health was wearing one. I stood in the bright sunshine waiting for my time to speak until someone came over with an umbrella to give me some shade. The speeches took twice as long as expected because they had to be translated into French. By the time my speech was over my clothes were soaked in sweat but I soon forgot that uncomfortable feeling when a massive group of mothers with their children surge forward to get the vaccination.

"I call that trip a "goose bump" experience," Marlene said.

A Rotarian snapped a photograph of Marlene putting the drops of vaccine into a baby's mouth. That photograph has appeared in numerous Rotary marketing campaigns for PolioPlus.

"This mother pushed her way through the crowd with her baby to get close to me so I could administer the drops," Marlene recalled. "She and the other mothers were just so happy we were there."

Our group flew to different parts of the Ivory Coast and saw thousands of children lined up to get the vaccination. There were 3.5 million kids immunized there in two days.

"I will never forget all of those big brown eyes and wide smiles showing rows of white teeth on those precious children as they waited their turn," Marlene said.

Jim Lacy made several trips to India and other countries to help immunize children.

"It's a feeling all of its own; it's something that just to put those two drops in that child's mouth and know that you are saving them from the dreaded disease of polio is just ...well it is just exhilarating really," he said.

By 1994, the Western Hemisphere was declared polio-free. The Western Pacific region, stretching from Australia to China, was declared polio-free in 2000.

While these milestones with polio eradication were taking place, I also started a program called the Russian Health Initiative (which I'll talk about more in Chapter 6). I had hoped to get the Gates Foundation based in Seattle to donate a $150,000 grant to that cause but had a hard time getting a meeting with Bill Gates, Sr., who oversaw the foundation at the time and was a Seattle Rotarian.

Then Ralph Munro, who served as Secretary of State for Washington for five terms and was past president of Seattle's Rotary, set up a meeting. Jim Lacy wanted to speak to Bill Gates, Sr., about grants for future Rotary projects. I went with him to Seattle to ask about a possible grant for the Russian Health Initiative.

But I quickly learned the request for $150,000 for the health initiative was small potatoes. The Gates Foundation was donating much larger sums of money to causes they chose and at that time the Russian Health Initiative was not among their interests. But how grateful both Jim and I were a few years later when Bill Jr. and Melinda Gates learned more about Rotary's campaign for polio eradication through their foundation leaders.

They sent a foundation representative to our Rotary convention and in 2007 the Bill & Melinda Gates Foundation issued a $100 million grant challenge to raise funds for polio eradication. In other words, if Rotary raised $100 million they would match it, which happened.

Two years later, the Gates Foundation gave Rotary an additional $255 million for polio eradication work and increased the challenge to $200 million. The foundation would match every $1 we raised with $3.55. By 2012, Rotary had exceeded the $200 million challenge and had raised $228 million. The following year the Gates Foundation pledged to match Rotary's contributions 2-to-1 up to $35 million per year for five years.

"Rotary in particular has inspired my own personal commitment to get deeply involved in achieving (polio) eradication," Bill Gates Jr. told Rotary officials. "The world wouldn't be where it is without Rotary, and it won't be where it needs to go without Rotary."

In 2015, Time magazine recognized Rotary's commitment. "For more than a generation, it has been Rotary that has led the drive to eradicate polio," the magazine reported.

Rotary and its partners were able to succeed because at each National Immunization Day volunteers learned lessons how to make the work

"Rotary is the heart and soul of polio eradication!"
– *Bill Gates*

even more efficient. For example, in the early days we did not paint each child's fingernail after getting the vaccination so in the confusion we would not vaccinate the child twice. This didn't harm the child but it did impact the overall number we could immunize.

Rotary also expanded the places vaccinations were given to include train and bus stations and airports. We wanted to expand the net as far as we could to reach as many children as possible.

In India, volunteers immunized 150 million kids in one weekend. Organizers set it up that for every six blocks in the city there was a stand where you could go and take your kids. They would also knock on doors and neighborhoods where they thought people were not coming out.

Each time Rotary had a National Immunization Day they reached at least 96 percent of the children.

Of course, there was resistance in some countries. Religious zealots, like the Taliban in Afghanistan and Pakistan, spread rumors that the polio vaccination was a ploy from the U.S. government to sterilize children to limit population in these Third World countries.

But our Rotarians in these foreign countries continue to work hard to educate their populations. For example, the town in Pakistan where Osama bin Laden was tracked down and killed has a very active Rotary club and has helped vaccinate children there.

India, which had long been considered the epicenter of the disease, was a great success story. People like Saint Mother Teresa embraced Rotary and put up posters of her giving a child the vaccination with the message: "May God Bless you for saving our children from polio."

By 2014, India celebrated three years of being polio-free. The work with polio also helped with other infectious disease outbreaks worldwide. Nigeria used the lessons learned from polio eradication to help with an Ebola outbreak.

Reports show that 10 million children have been spared disability and 250,000 deaths from polio averted. The financial savings in keeping these children healthy is estimated at $50 billion over 25 years.

World leaders praised Rotary for helping to eradicate polio worldwide including Mother Teresa.

"Grant and I have both been doing this since 1985," Lacy said. "I just am absolutely amazed at where we started and where we are today. But you know we are going to make it and we just have to keep plugging; we just can't stop now. We spent too much money, too much time and effort, and we have to finish the job."

We know the Rotarians could never have accomplished this alone but we also know we have played a major role.

"The World Health Organization says that Rotary is really the soul of this eradication effort," Lacy said. "They could have never done it (alone). Because Rotary has something that no one else in the world has: we have 1.2 million Rotarians in 170 countries. And they are usually the movers and shakers in all of these communities." Those Rotarians are called "troops on the ground."

In addition to working on the PolioPlus Advisory Committee I got more involved in Rotary International from the mid-1980s and served on several Rotary International committees including: Finance Committee, chairman for one year; Health & Hunger Task Force; Audit & Operations Review Committee, three-year term; Russian Health Initiative, chairman of task force for several years; Chairman 1st Russian Peace Initiative Conference, Anchorage, Alaska; and Co-chairman 2nd Russian Peace Conference , St. Petersburg, Russia.

In 1993, I was elected as one of 17 Rotarians worldwide to serve on the Rotary International Board for two years. This was the first time in 30 years a director had been chosen from this part of the world.

Over the years, my eyes had been opened to the rest of the world and my education was through Rotary. When I was elected as district governor, I attended a training session with the 530 other district governors from 170 countries. We gathered at a resort in Florida and had programs and discussions about the needs in their communities.

As we listened many of us decided to team up and work on projects to-gether. There was a wide range of things from at-risk youth to education and health issues. So, it is a tremendous interchange that goes on a regular basis every year among these Rotarians.

Everyone says that week is one of the best life changing experiences they ever had because we learn more about the world. As a Rotary International Director, I attended an International Assembly where all of these governors came together. I was in the receiving line and probably shook the hands of nearly 1,000 people, which included the 530 district governors and their wives. Getting to know the Rotarians throughout the world broke down racial and cultural stereotypes and opened my eyes even more to the world's problems.

This education included Russia, which for the majority of my life was seen as a great threat to the United States. In the late 1980s, my misconceptions about Russia were cleared up first through a Russian interpreter who attended the University of Denver and then through my travels to Moscow, Russia to help charter the first Russian Rotary Club in June 1990.

Chapter 6

Chartering 1st Russian Rotary and Russian Health Initiative

Opening our eyes to the Cold War enemy

Jim Lacy and I traveled together when I helped charter the first Rotary club in Russia. We joke because Marlene lent Jim her umbrella when we were in Moscow and she has never gotten it back.

"That is an ongoing joke with us," Marlene said. "We had two umbrellas and I had a raincoat so I gave Jim, who was wearing a suit, my umbrella."

My interest in Russia began several years before that trip when former Colorado Governor Richard Lamm, who had appointed me to the Colorado Highway Commission, began teaching at the University of Denver. He called me about a Russian woman, a translator, who was hoping to attend D.U. Lamm thought my connections with the Alumni Association may help.

Like many Americans at the time, I had a distorted view of Russia. After years of the Cold War, the image the media projected of Russian women was they were fat peasants who swept the streets. That image changed for me after Lamm introduced Marlene and me to Irina Chernova. In Moscow, Irina had started a freelance interpreter business for American businesses that wanted to do business in Russia as the Iron Curtain started to come down.

Several of the American business owners suggested Irina come to the United States and do the same translation work for Russian business owners visiting America. So, in 1989 she came to California and ended up in Denver where she met Dick Lamm. DU was thrilled to welcome Irina to

Colorado Governor Richard Lamm, sitting, was a member of Denver Rotary and also appointed me to serve on the Colorado Department of Highways Board of Directors. In this 1981 photo he met with me, left, and Stu Moore, executive director of Denver Rotary Club. Gov. Lamm hosted a meal at the governor's mansion each year for the Artist of America show and sale. We also worked together on projects involving the University of Denver.

their campus because the university had not had a Russian student in 50 years. She received a full-ride scholarship and she lived for a short time with a fellow Rotarian's family while also continuing her translation job for visiting Russian business owners.

Marlene and I helped Irina adjust to her new home and would take her shopping or have her to dinner. We also brought her to Rotary meetings a few times. She met her future husband – a visiting executive from a Russian uranium company – during one of her interpreting jobs in Colorado and they moved back to Russia.

Around the same time Irina was living in Denver, Russian president Mikhail Gorbachev was trying to move his country into the modern world. He learned about Rotary International and wanted to get Rotary clubs started in Russia.

He contacted Rotary officials and even traveled to Rotary headquarters in Illinois. But in those initial talks, Mr. Gorbachev insisted that every Russian Rotary club would have to allow a member of the Communist

During the Cold War, the stereotypical Russian woman was depicted to the West as being large and homely. We discovered that the Russian women are beautiful.

Party to attend the meetings. Rotary officials knew Rotary would benefit Russia but they couldn't agree to those terms. Each Rotary club must be independent of local government control.

Everyone left that meeting disappointed but Gorbachev decided he couldn't let this go. He later called Rotary and agreed to no restrictions. I was chairman of the Rotary International Finance Committee in 1990 and thrilled when I was chosen to help charter the first Russian Rotary club in Moscow. Also invited were about 15 other Rotarians from Sweden, Norway, England and Germany and a nucleus from the U.S. We had to pay our own travel expenses but we were excited to be part of the charter committee.

But right before Marlene and I were scheduled to leave on this historic trip, a huge hail storm hit our new home and shattered many of the clay tiles on our roof. Luckily, our windows weren't broken but we had a big mess on our hands.

Still, we knew we couldn't pass up this trip so we put the cleanup on hold and headed to Russia. We were excited but also a little apprehensive about the trip. At the time, it wasn't easy to fly into Russia. We took a plane to Stockholm and then another to Moscow.

The Russians had recruited 25 men to be in the first chartered club. They also recruited other Russians not involved in the charter group to greet us at the airport and bring us to dinner at their apartment before taking us to the hotel where the rest of our group was staying.

So, that trip was our baptism to Moscow. We soon discovered that the country was in real economic trouble. There was no available food at most of the stores. We couldn't find any restaurant to eat other than our hotel. The night of the charter dinner we had a beautiful spread with many delicious plates but we knew that was unusual because most of the city was surviving on minimal food options.

But ironically enough the first McDonald's in Russia opened while we were there and there were people a block long waiting in line, along with armed police and guards surrounding the building.

We had a lovely time at the charter dinner but six of the Russians who would be members of the first Russian Rotary Club were not at the meal for an important reason. They had traveled with Gorbachev to the U.S. to discuss the nuclear disarmament treaty.

Even though Communism was on the way out in Russia, it was clear to us that the majority of our original Rotary members had been members of the Party. The men looked like KGB people but they were friendly and their wives were very gracious hosts and beautiful women.

While we enjoyed the trip, we were glad when the airplane showed up and were headed to the comforts of our home.

The first Russian charter club had 25 members and within a year that had grown to 110 with a long waiting list. Many Russians saw their membership in Rotary as a door to the outside world and they wanted to join.

The second Russian Rotary club began in St. Petersburg. We started in Moscow and St. Petersburg because that area of the country is the most populated. Then our Rotary club in Anchorage, Alaska started helping to set up Rotary clubs in Siberia because geographically this area was closer to the United States. That allowed Rotarians in Alaska and Canada to easily help the Siberians set up their Rotary clubs.

While the Russian clubs were forming we thought it would be good to gather as many members as we could to discuss Russian issues with our other Rotarian members.

In 1995, I was the chairman of the "Russian Peace and Development Forum" in Anchorage. I worked with Steve Yoshida, a district governor in Alaska, in preparing the event.

"You, Steve Yoshida and your committee deserve every accolade for designing a conference that permitted us to share with like-thinking Rotarians from thirteen different countries in assessing the wishes of the new Russian Rotarians," World President Herbert G. Brown wrote in the conference's booklet.

"Concepts were revised and brotherly love was abundant as we spread our message of service, love and peace to our new friends," Brown wrote. "This was only possible because of your efforts."

The Russian Rotarians also were pleased with the conference.

"Each participant became spiritually richer having enjoyed a real Rotarian fellowship, having been brought together, having been a member, a part of a big family," wrote Kapa Alexeyeva, secretary of the Rotary Club of Yakutsk, Russia.

In 1997, we attended the Rotary International Peace Conference in St. Petersburg, Russia.

In 1997, I was the chair of Rotary's first "Peace Conference" in St. Petersburg and worked with Lennart Arfwidsson, a past Rotary International Director from Sweden.

"Less than a decade ago it was inconceivable that there would be Rotary clubs in Russia and throughout all of Eastern and Central Europe," World President Glen W. Kinross wrote in that program. "I believe this conference was an important step to improve cooperation among Rotarians of different nations, and will inspire many Rotarians to engage in International Service. Once again let me thank you and congratulate you for all of your effort."

We spoke about many topics at those two gatherings including the health needs of Russia.

During our first trip to Russia, Marlene and I saw firsthand how poor the medical services were for the country that had been shut off from the rest of the world for decades. We accompanied the English Rotarians from our Russian charter group who had an ambulance sent to Moscow that they donated to a small health clinic.

"The clinic had only one doctor and one older lady that was a nurse," Marlene recalled. "I don't think there were more than six or seven patients there. One patient was a lady from Chechnya whose leg had been blown off. The only medicine they had was a box of aspirin and nothing else. She started to scream when she saw us. We asked them what was wrong and they told us she was afraid that we had come to take her back to Chechnya."

Later, with the help of Rotarian Jim Lacy we set up a meeting in St. Petersburg with the Russian Minister of Health and some Russian Rotarians. We learned the Russians suffered from a variety of health problems, including epidemics of tuberculosis, HIV-AIDS and hypertension. Russians also lacked access to simple medical tests for diabetes and other treatable diseases.

It was such a big country and the medical needs seemed overwhelming. However, I had benefited from seeing the positive impacts of a community health fair started in Denver by a local television station, an NBC affiliate, and reportedly the world's oldest and largest community health fair.

The roots of the 9Health Fair were planted after a Dr. John Bensike, a physician studying heart disease research with the National Institutes of

My favorite building in Russia was this Orthodox Church in St. Petersburg.

Health in Washington, D.C., urged communities to educate residents about the importance of cholesterol screenings and medical follow-up. In the late 1970s, Al Flanagan, the president of KBTV Channel 9 in Denver, now 9NEWS, agreed to provide financial and media support to launch the first health fair in Denver.

The first 9Health Fair took place in 1980 with the support of hundreds of medical and non-medical volunteers, the Colorado National Guard and the Lions Clubs of Colorado. As news of the benefits of the health fair spread, the event expanded statewide with the help of 16,000 volunteers. It provides 25 screenings for a variety of health issues for free or low costs with follow-ups from doctors and nurses. 9Health Fair officials estimate the annual event has impacted more than 1.7 million Colorado residents.

Several years later, as a member of Rotary International's Health, Hunger and Humanity Program (3-H), I helped start the Russian Health Initiative – patterned after 9Health Fairs – and was chair of the program for several years. I helped get a $330,000 3-H Grant to help the 149 Russian Rotary Clubs start their health fairs.

The grant money also was used by Steve Yoshida and his Alaskan Rotarians. He had fielded requests from Russian clubs for donations to buy medicine and medical equipment.

"It was a hole impossible to fill," Yoshida recalled. "We could spend a lifetime trying to raise money with little impact. Maybe there was a better way."

The Homer Kachemak Rotary in Alaska had sponsored a similar health fair to 9Health Fair where they offered residents medical tests from hearing to blood sugar every year. They invited members of Russian Rotary clubs to the Homer Health Fair and they were able to set up health fairs in several Russian communities.

With our combined efforts, by 2007 there were more than 100 health fairs, mostly in Siberia and in eastern Russia. The Russian government acknowledged the benefits of the health fairs and started providing funding.

While the Russian Health Initiative was underway, other Russian exchange programs were starting in the U.S. Library of Congress Librarian James Billington started the Russian Leadership Program, which later was named "Open World." Billington had a great interest in the country and spoke Russian fluently. He had heard about Rotary's programs in Russia and thought it would be great to begin a program to introduce Russian citizens to the U.S. His idea was to ask Congress for about $6 million to start the program. I served as Rotary's representative to the Library of Congress.

Denver Rotarians hosted a group of Russians for about 10 days and they stayed in Rotarians' homes instead of hotels. We wanted them to really see how Americans lived. We paired the visitors to coincide with the Russian's professions, so Russian lawyers were paired with Rotarian lawyers and the same with doctors, bankers and merchants.

We met the Russians at Denver International with their Rotarian host families. Every day, the Russians would accompany the Denver Rotarians to their workplace and spent time with their host families. The goal was to show Russians our lifestyles while also forging friendships that would help the countries better understand each other.

So, I thought it would be a great idea to do the same kind of trip with Russian doctors to learn about the 9Health Fair. Our Denver Rotarians housed 36 participating doctors and every morning we had volunteers drive them to a health fair station in a different part of the city. We did this for the full week of the 9Health Fair so that they would see how it operated at the city parks, office buildings and other sites citywide.

Marlene helped drive the doctors to the 9Health Fairs and other fun activities we had planned during the week. We introduced them to Project CURE when we stopped by their medical equipment warehouse. Project C.U.R.E. (Commission on Urgent Relief and Equipment) identifies,

In 2008, a group of Russian doctors came to Denver at Rotary's invitation to learn more about the 9Health Fair.

solicits, sorts, and distributes medical supplies and services to communities worldwide.

James Jackson, father of Doug Jackson, a past president of the Rotary Club of Denver, founded the non-profit in 1987. I asked Doug to explain the organization in his own words, which follow.

"Like so many iconic organizations in America, Project C.U.R.E. was launched from a garage. Our garage was in a small Colorado mountain town, and my father had purchased it in the 1970's when he was rich. He had made his fortune in real estate, developing ski areas before it was popular. And my successful father and my beautiful mom, Anna Marie, made a profound discovery somewhere on the way to the bank. They discovered that you can be rich and not happy. So they gave it all away — to churches and colleges. My dad started doing economic consulting as a way of helping people with the lessons he had learned.

"It was in Brazil that he met an opportunity that would change his life − and mine - and the lives of hundreds of thousands of people around the world. His interpreter was a medical student. She and her mom would provide volunteer healthcare on the weekends to the poor people in Rio de Janeiro. She invited him to a small clinic operated in an old house in the middle of one of the poorest parts of the city. A long line of people stretched around the block in the hot sun, only to find there was nothing there for them. It tore my dad's heart out. Returning to Denver, he contacted some of his friends. Greg had a medical company and offered to donate medical supplies. My parents filled their garage, and shipped a semi-truck sized container to Brazil. That was the start.

"I am an attorney. I have a PhD in Finance. My goal was a large Manhattan office and only a dollar more than I could spend. Somewhere, my dad asked for help. We were awarded a small grant of $75,000 to pay my salesman buddy David, my runway model friend Doreen and me to help my pop. In six months, we had projected to run out of money, and thought we would need to find something else to do. That was 1997. And in between, something very remarkable has happened.

"Our little garage experiment has changed the world. From Albania to Zimbabwe, we have used the vehicle of donated medical supplies and equipment to save hundreds of thousands of people who wouldn't otherwise have a safety net; people who die from lack of a $4 pack of suture, who arrive at a clinic to learn that the doctor has no gloves, or who develop fatal cardiac conditions because they didn't have the tools to control a simple fever. It happens − all too often.

"For example, the rate of maternal mortality in most of the developed world hovers around 4 percent to 7 percent. In the places we work, it can be as high as 500 percent or more. The tragedy is that the announcement of an expectant mother is Russian roulette for most families − with four rounds in the chamber. But a significant intervention in the form of gloves, suture, an ambo-bag, a delivery table, beds and a few pieces of infant equipment to provide heat and oxygen will reverse those tragic statistics − sometimes by half. We know that because we have seen it first-hand. Where Project C.U.R.E. has placed the tools for health into the hands of trained healthcare workers, miraculous transformations have occurred. Suffering is reduced and lives are saved.

"At the same time, we have watched tens of thousands of people come to Project C.U.R.E. every year to volunteer. Some will sort the medical supply donations and pack them into boxes. Other people will help to repair medical equipment, match it with the cords, cables and consumables necessary to make it all work correctly. Each forty-foot container is loaded one box at a time until there is no more room from top to bottom, side to side. These containers, the size of semi-truck trailers are delivered by boat to the port and then trucked to the recipient hospital. The exact content of the container is determined by an on-site Needs Assessment study, which is also conducted by volunteers. We even created an opportunity for nurses and doctors to travel with Project C.U.R.E. and provide hands-on medical care in our C.U.R.E. Clinics program. Throughout the process, volunteers from the U.S. have intervened to re-write history for enough people to fill a football stadium many times over."

So, when we brought the Russian doctors to Project C.U.R.E.'s warehouse in Denver, they were amazed and in awe of what they saw. It houses medical supplies for doctors, dentists and surgeons from wall to wall.

"Some of that stuff is old compared to what we have in the United States," Marlene recalled. "One of the Russian doctors was a dentist and spotted an item that to me looked like an antique. He got so excited. He asked if he could have it and take it in his suitcase and I said yes you can take anything you can get through customs. But I couldn't help but think I was glad I wasn't his patient."

Other Russian doctors also took items that they could carry and were like children on Christmas morning looking at the equipment that would make a huge difference in their patients' lives.

We also took the Russian doctors to see the world renowned Western art collection of Phil Anschutz. The American Museum of Western Art, across from the famous Brown Palace Hotel in downtown Denver, displays 350 pieces of Anschutz's collection. The Russian doctors didn't seem that impressed because they didn't understand the significance of the collection showing the history of the American West. However, later that night I got a call from the galley curator who remembered she had several boxes of books in Russian about the collection. Anschutz had the books made when the art collection had been displayed earlier in Russia at the Hermitage Museum in St. Petersburg.

On the last day, we gathered the Russian doctors from their host families in Denver and loaded them on a bus to Estes Park. We wanted to let them see our majestic mountains and wildlife then later we drove them to a hotel near the airport so it would be easy for them to depart together. On the bus drive, I got on the loud speaker and told them we had a gift for them. When they were able to read about the art in their Russian language, they finally understood the Anschutz collection. They became excited and animated, almost as much as when they visited Project C.U.R.E.

The Russian Health Initiative helped address many medical needs with the health fairs and our Denver Rotarians continued to support the Russian needs through Project C.U.R.E. However, one of the first shipments of medical equipment to Russia did not go as planned.

When Jim Jackson began Project C.U.R.E. he insisted on visiting each community personally before any medical items were shipped. He did this to assess the needs of the clinic or hospital and also if the locals could protect the items from falling into the wrong hands. If criminals – or corrupt government officials – intercepted the medical equipment, they could sell the items on the black market. So, Jim and later Doug had people on the ground that they trusted to get the items safely to the health centers.

Rotary clubs throughout Colorado helped support Project C.U.R.E. and one year the president of the Denver Club of Rotary agreed to accompany the medical supplies to Russia.

"When we got ready to deliver the stuff we did it with Russian Rotarians at the other end so that the Russian mafia didn't get the medical supplies and sell the items," my brother, Jim, recalled.

My brother and his wife were initially to go on the trip with our club president at the time, Joan Bristol, but they had non-refundable tickets for a cruise planned before the Russian trip.

"Joan got over there before the plane arrived and found out the mafia was going to receive the supplies and never give them to the hospitals," Jim said. "So, she got on the phone. She had a lot of guts. She really risked her life, I think, because she got on the phone and called the plane off. She kept it from landing there and the mafia backed down. Once the local Rotarians got control of the situation, she allowed the plane to deliver the items and the Russian Rotarians made sure the medical supplies got to the right people."

Unfortunately, there are people who try and take advantage of organizations trying to help the world but the key is to find ways to crush those efforts and continue to move forward.

My work with Rotary in Russia interested my friend, Carl W. Reddel, while he was a Brigadier General with the United States Air Force based in Colorado Springs. Reddel, who retired and now serves as the executive director of the Dwight D. Eisenhower Memorial Commission, recalled our work together.

"I came to Rotary International by way of Russia because of Grant Wilkins. As a Russian-speaking American military officer, who had worked in successful collaboration with Soviet officers to destroy nuclear-capable missiles during the Cold War, I had found that turning swords into plowshares was not simple and not readily done, as Grant and other Rotarians know."

"Before meeting Grant, I did not know about Rotary's long-standing international efforts in this regard. Neither did I know how Rotarians were attempting to address the human suffering left by the enormous void created and not addressed by the ineffectiveness and inaction of the world's governments during and following the Cold War."

"Huge numbers of people, traumatized and harmed by the global rivalry and conflict of the two nuclear super powers, were on their own in their own countries and globally. But thanks to Grant's leadership and the support of other Rotarians, Cold War healing began in Russia after the Cold War and continues to this day."

"As a professional military officer, I have learned that Rotary's noble activities in Cold War healing and Grant's humane leadership are not solely "do-good, feel-good" charitable acts. They are rooted in the twin, combined underpinnings of democratic values and valid geopolitical certainties, which dramatically increases their significance."

Rotary's success in setting up health fairs in Russia encouraged me to work with the people in Fiji, including our island of Wakaya. I contacted Rotarians in Fiji and they chose two people who came to Denver to learn about the 9Health Fair. Several areas of Fiji had limited health care because many villages are located in isolated mountains and valleys.

I took two members of Denver Rotary who were doctors to Fiji to help with the first health fair there. We had no idea what to expect and were quite pleased when about 1,500 people showed up. Once the local people were trained, the health fairs became very popular and spread throughout the country.

While the health fairs remain active in Russia, our Russian Rotary clubs have faced some growing pains. Like the country itself, we've seen divisions between generations on how things should be run and that's hurt the overall membership.

My hope is that some of the stronger Russian Rotarians find a way to fill the gap and revitalize the clubs. One of the younger members, Andrei Danilenko, became our friend and we still keep in touch. He is a dual citizen of Russia and the U.S. and became our first Rotary International District Governor in Western Russia.

Andrei Danilenko, right, became our first Rotary International District Governor in
Western Russia. He is a dual citizen of Russia and the U.S. and is our friend.

Andrei was born in Moscow but came to America with his mother
who became a teacher at the University of California at San Diego. His
father remained in Russia and Andrei returned as a young adult and later
became a Russian Rotarian. He's now a major player in the agriculture
industry there, and is an adviser to Russian President Vladimir Putin and
the Russian government regarding agriculture and raising cattle.

When I last saw Andrei in 2014 he was farming 330,000 acres and had
45,000 head of cattle for both dairy products and beef.

Russian Rotarians, like Andrei, can reunite the membership but we
know it will take time. Meanwhile, other Rotarian clubs worldwide
continue to grow.

At our 2016 world convention in Korea there were so many Korean
Rotarians that they had to have extra sessions. All of the sessions are
translated because Rotarians who attend are from all corners of the world.

There's also a growing interest in China for Rotary, although we still have an issue of government officials insisting Communists attend the meetings, which we still don't allow. I think like Russia that condition will eventually be removed and Rotary clubs there will become very popular once we can officially charter the clubs. As of 2016, we have a few provisional clubs made up of ex-pats and foreign citizens living in China.

Marlene and I continued to learn more about other countries by attending 26 world conventions of Rotary International: 13 in foreign countries and 13 in the United States. In years past, the U.S. had half of the world's Rotarians but now that is less than 30 percent. But I am not discouraged by the drop in American Rotarians. I believe that as more young people get involved, the numbers will grow. As with each generation, some things will change but the heart of Rotary – community service – will continue to be strong.

Another avenue that I have learned more about the world and other cultures is through my work with the University of Denver Alumni Association. I reconnected with the university when I was asked to serve as district chief for my Beta Theta Pi Fraternity. In addition to D.U., I oversaw the fraternity chapters at the University of Colorado in Boulder, Colorado College in Colorado Springs and the Colorado School of Mines in Golden.

I basically counseled the young fraternity men. It was a volunteer job and I enjoyed reconnecting with the university and its students. And D.U. traditionally had a strong connection with the Rotary Club of Denver because all of the past presidents and chancellors of the university were club members. Former D.U. Chancellor Chester Alter served as club president in 1958-59.

I later also was asked to serve as chairman of the Chancellor Society at D.U. and that increased my activities. Marlene and I attended annual dinners on campus and started donating money to the university on a regular basis.

Former D.U. Chancellor Dan Ritchie really made a huge impact on the university. He donated his own money and raised more than any other chancellor to enhance and expand the programs at D.U. Ritchie's work continued when former D.U. Chancellor Bob Coombe took over. Bob became a good friend and I got him into Rotary. Their work has made D.U. one of the Top 10 universities in the U.S.

D.U. has become such a prestigious institute that students need to go through an interview process as part of their application. For every 12 applications, there is only one slot. I have served on the interviewing committee in Denver; there are 30 different interviewing sites nation-wide. The students have to be in the top 10 percent of their class even to be considered a candidate to apply.

The university also is popular with international students. I initially wasn't particularly interested in The Josef Korbel School of International Studies on campus. It was established in 1964 and offers undergraduate, graduate and doctoral degrees for international students. It was named in honor of founding dean, Josef Korbel, father of former U.S. Secretary of State Madeleine Albright. Josef Korbel also taught another famous D.U. student, former U.S. Secretary of State Condoleezza Rice.

In 2016, there were 1,291 international students enrolled at D.U. from 92 countries. The students at the Korbel School have studied such programs as international human rights, global trade, international administration and conflict resolution. Many of the students enroll after serving in the Peace Corps.

I met the dean of the school, Chris Hill, a former U.S. ambassador, who worked as a Peace Corps volunteer in Cameroon and ambassador to Macedonia, Poland, South Korea and Iraq. He was a member of the team that negotiated the Bosnia peace settlement and has worked on negotiations with North Korea.

I was a member of the Beta Theta Pi Fraternity at the University of Denver when I attended school. Later, I served as the district chief for the fraternity and traveled to fraternity conventions including 1975 in Michigan to meet with fraternity members.

Chris impressed me so much that I started to learn more about the Korbel School. It became clear the school's mission to promote world peace by educating international students aligns with the goals of Rotary.

It was quite an honor when on September 8, 2015 I received the Josef Kobel Humanitarian of the Year award for my work on PolioPlus. President George W. Bush was given the award in 2013 for his work on the AIDS crisis.

It was touching to celebrate with friends and family at the awards dinner, which included Denver Mayor Michael Hancock, Governor John Hickenlooper and U.S. Secretary of Defense Chuck Hagel.

"Thank you for being the person you are," former D.U. Chancellor Bob Coombe said in a video made of the evening.

111

When Marlene and I sold our condo in Santa Fe, N.M, we used some of the proceeds to establish an annual scholarship to be awarded to a student attending the Korbel School. We wanted to do this while we are still able to enjoy meeting the recipients and learning about their lives, rather than having the scholarship established after our deaths. The college added to our donation and the scholarship should be awarded yearly for many years.

I'm very proud when I can merge my dedication to D.U. and Rotary and that happened in July 2010.

Denver Rotary Club 31 launched the Collegiate International Student Engagement Program as a pilot initiative undertaken by the club's new members. First partnering with D.U. through its Office of Alumni Relations, the project is designed to encourage Rotary Club 31 members to engage international students enrolled at Denver area colleges and universities in an effort to make them feel welcomed in their new community.

We kicked off the program with a luncheon at D.U. with 75 international students and Rotarians. Then another 50 international students joined us at a Club 31 meeting. The pilot program was adopted by D.U. and many other Rotary Clubs are so impressed how well the program has worked they want to start one of their own.

Through this program, Rotary members are sharing the vision and mission of Rotary International with the objectives of fostering a desire in the students to be active in Rotary when they return to their home country and enter the business arena. This program is one that every Rotary Club in the world that has a college or university within its area can create, and I am proud my alma mater is supporting it.

I got to meet many international students at D.U., including a Chinese student named Jacky Song. There are about 750 Chinese students at D.U. and Jacky was very outgoing and was invited to attend student leadership conferences. I gave a talk about Rotary at one of those conferences and Jacky came up to me afterwards and said he wanted to be a Rotarian.

I explained that would be a great idea after he graduated and worked a couple of years.

From that conversation, Jacky and I formed a friendship and he got to know Marlene, too. He calls us his "American grandparents." We attended his graduation from D.U. with honors and a business degree in accounting. His father works in China as a city attorney for a city of about seven million residents. They wanted to give Jacky a BMW as a graduation present but he wanted a Honda Accord. At 24, he had his first driving experience on Denver streets.

Jacky worked for the large accounting firm KPMG in Denver with a great starting salary but they worked him 12 hours a day. Interestingly enough, one of his assignments required him to audit the Navajo Nation and I ended up introducing him to Tony Davis, the son of my Navajo Indian friend Roger Davis, who I met while in the sign business.

After working in Denver for two years, he transferred to KPMG's Chicago office so he could pursue a M.B.A. at the University of Chicago.

Denver Rotary also has another program at D.U. called Rotaract, a service club for the students. This program focuses on volunteer service,

I have stayed active with the University of Denver since I graduated in 1947. In 2007, Marlene and I attended my 50th class reunion.

leadership, professional development and international understanding and goodwill. In addition, D.U. sends about 70 percent of its students abroad each year to study in their specific field and learn about a new culture. D.U. ranked third in the country for undergraduate participation in the study abroad program in 2016.

The D.U. students have a choice of about 120 foreign universities to study at and there is no additional cost. The tuition they pay for a four-year degree at D.U. includes this wonderful opportunity.

These partnerships with D.U. and Denver Rotary allow young adults to learn more about the world and in turn, hopefully, move toward world peace.

As I learned more about D.U. over the years, I also have learned more about world problems through my friendships with other Rotarians. I had one particular enlightening conversation with Rotarian Steve Werner several years ago when he mentioned another serious problem is the lack of clean water worldwide.

Chapter 7

Clean Water & Child Immunization in the U.S.

Our continued missions

I know you are never too old to learn new things or take on a new challenge.

In 2003, I spoke to the American Water Works Association Convention in Anaheim, California on PolioPlus. And while I educated their membership on polio eradication worldwide, they educated me about the lack of clean water worldwide.

At the height of the polio epidemic an estimated 1,000 people a day were infected and 100 people died daily from the virus. Those are astounding numbers.

So, I was caught off guard when I learned that 6,000 people a day worldwide died because of illnesses caused by unclean water. At the time, I had no idea about those high fatality numbers.

Rotary has a long history of working on community water and sanitation issues. In 1907, the Rotary Club of Chicago helped the city build public toilets. That work on unclean water eventually expanded to the more than 660 million people worldwide who live without safe drinking water and the nearly 40 percent of countries that have no sanitary toilet facilities.

Rotary International established a Water and Sanitation Rotarian Action Group, WASH RAG. In fact, the group's slogan is "start with water." When I chaired the Task Force on Health and Hunger and Humanity, I served as an adviser on the Water Task Force.

I never could have done all the work I did for PolioPlus without the support of Marlene. Whether it was traveling the world to give children vaccinations, or speaking to Rotary clubs nationwide, Marlene was always at my side.

Denver Rotarians had clean water projects in the Philippines, India and other countries but I didn't understand the magnitude of the problem until that AWWA convention. The person who invited me to speak at the convention was a fellow Rotarian Steve Werner. I had known Steve since 1989 when he joined Rotary. He worked for two worldwide non-profits before heading Water for People, an international program promoting clean water projects.

"Grant was surprised, like many Americans, to learn that the lack of clean water is such a big problem around the world," Werner said. "We just turn on a tap and clean water comes out and we don't think about the fact that most of the world does not have that luxury. After Grant learned how large of a problem it is, he said well we have to do something about it."

Steve and I knew Rotary could do even more projects than already were underway if we better educate members about the impact of unclean water. We did that by getting an article on clean water in the Rotarian magazine for its 1.3 million members and also by meeting with Rotary leadership.

"Grant, of course, had a lot of credibility because he worked on Polio-Plus," Werner said. "He literally took me by the hand to meet with the Rotary presidents at Evanston, at other meetings across the country and international conventions."

I made the introductions citing that 6,000 people a day died from unclean water illnesses and then handed it off to Steve to educate the Rotarians further about the need for us to focus on more clean water projects.

I urged all of Rotary's 33,000 clubs to undertake at least one clean water project.

"I was invited to speak at many Rotary district conferences and zone institutes," Werner said. "So, again I really believe it goes back to the fact that Grant paved the way for Rotarians to learn about this issue."

Rotary clubs have taken on more than 10,000 clean water projects worldwide with the numbers climbing each year. In partnership with USAID, Rotary clubs have built wastewater treatment plants in the Philippines, worked to improve sanitation in Ghana and developed water treatment and safe storage for homes in the Dominican Republic. And that is naming just a few of the ongoing water projects.

In 2015, Rotary allocated $20 million in 302 global grants to address water and sanitation needs worldwide. Yearly, thousands of Rotarians travel to communities worldwide to help build safe water wells for villages and small towns.

"I really can't thank Grant enough for wanting to do something and taking the initiative and explaining how to attack a big problem on an advocacy basis at multiple levels," Werner said.

I think clean water should be a top priority for Rotary because the lack of clean water affects communities in many different ways. For example, in some countries children won't go to school if they don't have access to close clean water. A community's workforce is impacted if workers get sick from unclean water and of course thousands of people die, including babies from simple diarrhea.

"I am passionate about clean water but I know many other Rotarians are passionate about literacy and other projects but all those needs do come together and intersect in communities," Werner said.

We also tried to get funding from a businessman and I went through a fellow Rotarian who ran the man's foundation. My fellow Rotarian didn't think this man would be interested in giving Rotary or Water for People a grant. But then The Denver Post sent a reporter and photographer to Africa with Steve Werner and wrote about the problems there.

The day after the story ran on the front page of the Post, my fellow Rotarian called me. He said his boss had given him a $10,000 check and wanted me to get it to Steve. That just goes to show you often have to talk to a person directly about a program than relying on his staff. You never know what someone may be interested in supporting.

We also learned that that like our PolioPlus program, local Rotarians need to be involved with the clean water projects over the long haul.

"Your first reaction may be let's go over there and build them a well," Werner said. "Well, that's only one part of the project because the community must know how to operate the well, maintain the well and fix the well."

And that brings me to a somewhat controversial issue that could affect our polio eradication issues. Polio was officially eradicated from the United States in 1974, which means many of our younger generations know little or anything about the disease.

In the U.S., the polio vaccine is usually given to children four times at age two months, four months, six-to-18 months and four-to-six years. Doctors often give this vaccination at the same time for other childhood illnesses like measles. But unfortunately in this age of the internet some parents get misinformed and worry vaccinations could harm their children. There even was a bogus report that some immunizations caused a spike in autism among children.

Now, there's no question where I stand on this. Every child needs to be immunized, period. Yet, my home state of Colorado has one of the worst rates of immunizing children in the country. For many years, the law was so lax that parents could opt out of vaccinating their children for religious or philosophical reasons.

And guess what? We had an outbreak of measles in our public schools. Rotary clubs in Denver and the surrounding suburbs saw this problem several years ago and started a program to educate parents called "Shots for Tots."

Urologist Frank Sargent, past District Governor of 5450, was a board member for Swedish Medical Center, which was celebrating its 100th anniversary and wanted to commemorate the milestone with a community project. (I had also served on the Swedish Medical Center board and will talk about that in Chapter 8.)

"The board fell in love with the idea and we worked with Swedish and the University Hills Rotary Club, the Denver Tech Center club, Englewood and Littleton clubs," recalled Sargent, a member of the Englewood Rotary Club.

These groups reached out to area health departments to inform parents of the need to immunize their children. Additionally, they worked with the local schools. Rotary sponsored a large vaccination clinic each year at a centrally located site for several years. But by 2008, the number of children taking advantage of the clinic dropped off and the program stopped.

My interest in the medical field included serving on the Swedish Medical Center Board of Trustees. I served for 20 years, including three years as chairman. We had numerous fundraisers for the hospital, including a Mardi Gras Ball celebration in 1988 where I was crowned their first Mardi Gras Ball King!

Public schools get funding based on the number of students in each school and there was reluctance to push the immunizations.

"In Colorado you know it's tough. It's not just medical reasons the families back away but its philosophical reasons," Sargent said.

But after the measles outbreak lawmakers got involved and in 2014 Colorado tightened the laws for opting out of vaccinations. Parents have to fill out more forms and have legitimate reasons for not immunizing their children. Additionally, the school districts have to report immunization rates to the state, which are available to the public.

My daughter, Shari, saw the problem firsthand when she worked as a public school principal.

120

"Oh I just think it is so scary when parents don't immunize their kids," Shari said. "When you don't know what polio is, you've never heard of it or have met someone with it, you don't know what it did to the whole American population."

Shari said the issue must be taken seriously because of the impact on all children.

"I just think it is crazy how historically we make advances, we get somewhere and then the next generation comes along and says well phooey on that without really understanding the deadly consequences," she said.

Shari speaks with college students and health professionals about the needs of gay senior citizens. Sometimes the topic of polio comes up for her to educate people about polio and the post-polio syndrome many seniors experience.

"I tell them you heard about AIDS in your lifetime," Shari said. "Well the AIDS in my lifetime was polio and it impacted a lot of people and they look at me like what?"

My son, Mark, has had the same reaction from younger generations never exposed to polio.

"Polio wasn't uncommon when I grew up," he recalled, saying he knows friends whose legs and arms were impacted by the virus. "When we took our mom out, we would get stares but people at that time understood polio and the impact it had."

Even in my family there was a brief discussion of the benefits of vaccinations before our oldest great-grandchild was immunized.

"Where I live there is a fair amount of people who don't immunize their kids," Mark said. "None of these parents in their 30s have any clue. They have never seen polio; they don't have any history of it; and they don't have any idea what it's like.

"My kids heard the stories," Mark said. "They have immunized the grandkids and I think for the most part they understand the importance of the immunizations because of their grandpa."

My fellow Rotarians also are concerned about the immunization rates in the U.S.

Steve Werner worked for the Children's Immunization Campaign before he joined Water for People.

"If your child is going to school with a child who has not been properly immunized your child is at risk," Werner said. "There are issues about the role of government but I think the bottom line is that we shouldn't put any children at-risk because the parents feel it is their right to make that decision.

"Again, I think that is where Rotary could play a big role," Werner said. "We can be on the front lines of telling the story and using the example of polio because eradicating polio is going to be a great gift to the world. This is an example of why it is so important to immunize our kids here from polio and many other diseases."

Rotarian John Klug agrees we can't take a step back in the U.S.

"We're just one plane ride away from an outbreak of polio in this country because we're very complacent," he said. "We're trying to immunize the rest of the world but we have a large population here that is relevant. While we are eradicating polio in the rest of the world we can't allow ourselves to be vulnerable here."

Peter I. Hartsock, captain of the U.S. Public Health Service, helped me when we were working on the Russian Health Initiative. He has closely studied the issue of children immunization. In 2014, he wrote the below letter that was published in the Washington Post. I believe parents should be aware of all of the implications of not vaccinating their children.

"The importance of vaccines is too often ignored, not understood or forgotten. We live in a strange time when many people are suspicious of a powerful means to prevent and eradicate disease," Peter wrote.

"A particularly important benefit of vaccination is its critical effect on the evolution of disease. A growing number of deadly maladies are becoming resistant to drugs. Every infection prevented through vaccines means less need for medical treatments for that type of infection. This, in turn, helps reduce the speed at which diseases "adapt" to and render medications ineffective.

"No country can afford to shell out money for treatments that lose their power, especially given the difficulty of developing new medications to take their place…Increased vaccination would not only prevent sickness and loss of life to disease but also help save the effectiveness of those treatments that we do have and that we may be stuck with for a long time. Benjamin Franklin's axiom that "An ounce of prevention is worth a pound of cure" is as relevant today as it ever was."

We need to heed Peter's advice and wise words because we can never take for granted that a child or adult in the U.S. will never suffer from polio again. When Marlene and I went to the Ivory Coast, we received the polio vaccination just to make sure we didn't catch or carry the virus home. It was purely precautionary but we can never be too cautious.

I received the International Service Award from Rotary International for a Polio-Free World and the PolioPlus Pioneer Award. But the greatest award will be when we can finally declare the world free of polio.

Another award that was quite humbling is when I was chosen in 2009 to receive the most prestigious award in Rotary: the Service Above Self award. This award is given to only 150 Rotarians worldwide each year.

Like my father, I take the mission of Rotary very seriously and to be honored this way was truly wonderful. I also strive to continue to look for projects that benefit the most people in our community. That's why when I was asked to chair a committee for the Rotary Club of Denver's 100th anniversary I wanted to find a project that benefited the largest number of people in the state of Colorado.

Chapter 8

Coloradans Can Thank Rotary for High-Speed Internet Access

*The Rotary Club of Denver's 100th anniversary
and Surviving Cancer*

When planning for the Rotary Club of Denver's 100th anniversary in 2011 our committee got several suggestions on what community project we should take on for this milestone.

My brother, Jim, suggested expanding Denver Kids and finding at least 100 new mentors. Others suggested we build a new homeless shelter in Denver or put our energies into helping victims of domestic violence.

All of those ideas were good but I and others felt we needed to do something that would help our entire state. The Rotary Club of Denver basically is the grandfather of all of the other Rotary clubs in Colorado because it was the first Rotary club in the state. And as a grandfather, we should spread out the benefits of celebrating our centennial year to all corners of the state.

So, I and others began investigating what was going on statewide. We discovered in the early years of the internet and high fiber optics that many regions of our state lacked internet access or what access they had was very slow. For example, if you lived on the Eastern Plains or high mountain towns you may not have access to the internet because the high fiber cables needed to bring internet into the communities was not available.

Some communities also were charged outrageous fees because of the limited access. Additionally, the lack of proper high fiber optics meant getting on the internet was terribly slow in many communities.

125

At that time, Colorado ranked 42nd out of 50 states in broadband connectivity and services were priced 10 times higher than neighboring states.

I learned about this from Rotarian John Klug who was one of the pioneers in creating internet web pages for businesses.

"Well I had spent the later part of my business career using the internet and developing web pages for the internet," Klug said. "I had a large internet company. So I had some knowledge through my work experience that Colorado was basically an economic duopoly: the phone company called US West, Qwest and now Centurylink provided DSL service and the internet over the phone. Then with Comcast you get internet through cable.

"They were the economic duopoly and they basically were charging exorbitant rates throughout the state, including to the school systems, and providing very poor service at a very slow speed. So, the children in the state were getting very poor service. The cost was on track to literally bankrupt some school systems in the state. It was a true crisis," Klug said.

Initially, we discussed a smaller Internet-related project with the Colorado History Museum, which was gearing up to open a new building downtown. They had wanted to open about 50 communication stations statewide that would provide internet access for students to learn about the state's history.

But then we heard about a larger project and we urged our members to get behind a program called EAGLE-Net Alliance, which aimed to bring Colorado schools out of the "dark ages" in terms of high-speed internet access and capacity.

"We discussed what we could do for our club's 100th anniversary that will last for perhaps 100 years and people will look back and say what a dramatic affect it had on the entire state," Klug said. "We had that as our prism and this need to wire the state and all the school systems with high speed internet seemed to fit those criteria."

Colorado's Centennial Board of Cooperative Education, a Long-mont-based non-profit that provided services to 14 school districts, suggested the public/private partnership with EAGLE-net (Educational Access Gateway Learning Environment).

The partnership would bring broadband, primarily through fiber optic cable, to 178 school districts statewide. The group, with the backing of several businesses, Colorado State University and the Colorado Department of Transportation raised $35 million and applied for a federal stimulus grant.

Before Rotary's involvement, the partnership's application for the $100 million federal grant for Colorado, which was part of President Obama's $7.2 billion broadband stimulus program, was denied. The group was told its application did not show enough community support for the project.

Well, I knew we could turn that around with my Rotary connections in all three districts in Colorado. Denver Rotary enlisted 8,499 members from 148 Rotary clubs statewide. We also got the support of Governor John Hickenlooper and a joint resolution from the Colorado Legislation.

We also asked Rotarians former Governor Dick Lamm and former Colorado Sen. Hank Brown to make a YouTube video that would help drum up support.

In July 2010, we posted that video and urged all of our Coloradan Rotarians to view it.

"The grant applications have had broad support from public officials, at both the federal and state level, but the reality is it needs support from the community as well. The intensity of the support makes a difference," Brown said on the video.

Denver Rotary's goal to get internet access to everyone in the state of Colorado required we replace large outdated fiber optic cables with smaller cables with higher speed.

A few months later, EAGLE-Net was awarded a $100.6 million grant and the group also garnered about $44 million from in-kind donations. But like with many federally-funded programs, it hit snags along the way.

But in the end the project was successful. All of the state's school systems got the high speed internet access which also is available to hospitals, libraries, public buildings and the community at-large.

"We did indeed wire the state with fiber to virtually every community in the state, some have to use microwave, but we brought high speed internet to every school in the state and about 850,000 students," Klug said.

While our initial goal was providing high-speed internet access to every school district in Colorado, we knew every resident would benefit because once the schools were wired the entire community was wired.

"We brought high speed internet access to four million people in Colorado. Actually many people in the state don't understand Rotary helped accomplish that," Klug said.

It's true that most people who live in Colorado have no idea Rotary is the reason the state is properly wired for high speed internet, but the school districts and others truly appreciated our involvement.

"I would tell you that it's been a positive story for our school districts in Colorado," Steve Clagg, president of the Colorado Association of Leaders in Educational Technology told the Denver Post in 2016. "Kids are getting access. It's improved the teaching environment, there is no doubt."

The Aurora School District, which borders Denver, reported it was able to cut its internet network costs by 60 percent over two years because of the project.

We knew that once the state was wired other groups and individuals would benefit so I feel the project was very successful. My daughter, Shari, explained that the high speed internet access also helps the gay community in being able to communicate with people statewide.

"Gay people in rural areas don't know where it's safe and who is safe," Shari explained. "We've been able to start a writing group that has gone international from Denver and we have people from all over the state who participate. When they didn't have access to private internet, they didn't feel comfortable going to a library."

"It was a wonderful outcome; not only for the schools but it's doing good for others," Shari said. "It's always good to focus on youth but if there's spill over somewhere else it has an even bigger impact."

We took on a risk when we got involved with a large project like EAGLE-Net and survived the criticism. But I think a Rotary group like ours needs to take risks if we believe in a project.

Another area I'd like to see Rotary get more involved is the health crisis of obesity in the United States. There is an epidemic of diabetes and other major health issues because of obesity. Reports show 25 percent of our elementary school students and 35 percent of high school students are overweight and one large problem is the lack of exercise.

I know that one reason I survived prostate cancer and throat cancer is that my wife, Marlene, got me interested in exercising early in our marriage. We both had been active hiking and skiing but it wasn't until Marlene was asked to join a YMCA by a woman who was our neighbor that we started a daily exercise routine.

"My neighbor and I went to the Y and they had neat exercise classes. It was so much fun," Marlene recalled. "After the Y we started to jog down the street or walk. No one was jogging then. We had the best time and loved going there. I told Grant let's just go out in the neighborhood and jog, we can do that. So we went up and down in our neighborhood. All of our neighbors probably thought what are those people doing? But that is how we really started our daily exercising. "

We moved from that home to another near the High Line Canal, which is a popular path through Denver's south suburbs that stretches for 71 miles through natural wildlife areas. We jogged until our knees started to feel the impact and then switched to walking.

Marlene and I usually walk two miles a day. And at 90 years old, I still do 30 push-ups a day. That's something I am proud of because most people years younger can't do 10 push-ups!

My family likes to tease me a little about my health routine but it has kept both of us healthy in our golden years.

"I once told someone my dad was my brother," Shari joked. "He does look a lot younger than his age."

Marlene also keeps an eye on our diet.

"Except on Saturday's when they go get donuts," quipped my brother, Jim.

I believe a major reason I have lived beyond 90 and survived polio and cancer is by keeping physically fit. Marlene and I love to visit the Estes Park area and in 1991 I caught a few fish at Elk Falls Ranch.

Marlene and I walk at least two miles a day and in 2016 we hiked the Gila Wilderness near Silver City, New Mexico.

One of the bakeries in our neighborhood has the best sticky buns and we do enjoy them on the weekend. I'm not preaching that people shouldn't enjoy their food but everyone should be conscious of their diet and exercise routines.

My interest in this area includes my work as a board member at Swedish Medical Center in Denver.

About the same time I joined the Rotary Club of Denver I became a board member at the hospital. That came about after Marlene and I took a photographic safari in Africa with other Denver residents.

There was a group called the English Speaking Union which had chapters all over the country to foster better relations between Britain and America. I had been a member before Marlene and I got married and on my first trip with the group I took Shari to Europe.

In 1969, we got a chance to go on this trip to Africa. The deal was if I got 20 other people to sign up, Marlene and I would have our trip expenses covered. We signed up the 20 people and then headed out on the six-week trip called The Best of Africa. It was an amazing adventure as we visited Kenya, Uganda, Tanzania and South Africa.

I didn't know many of my fellow travelers on the trip but one of the men was a Denver attorney Winston Howard of the law firm of Sherman & Howard, along with several others who were Rotarians. As we got to know each other on the trip, I learned that Howard was the most active and prominent member of the Swedish Medical Center board.

We forged a friendship with Winston and his wife over the six weeks of traveling and eating together. About a year later, he asked me to join the Swedish Medical Center board. I served for 20 years, which is the longest you can stay on the board. I was chairman of the board for three years.

We did some interesting things on that board, which included sending 12 doctors to China to learn about alternative medicine and enforcing the first smoking ban at the hospital.

The doctors at Swedish who made the trip saw some amazing things in China. They witnessed a heart transplant without anesthesia and instead using acupuncture. They also saw a young man have his appendix removed with acupuncture. When the operation was done the man stood up and walked out of the operating room. It was really amazing and opened my eyes to holistic medicine.

The doctors enjoyed the trip but I don't think it changed their minds very much. It's taken more than 40 years but I'm pleased to report that University of Colorado Cancer Center now has a regenerative medicine department, which opened in 2015. It offers chiropractic, massage therapy, acupuncture and other holistic treatments.

I practice what I preach and underwent both radiation and acupuncture treatments with my throat cancer.

My work on the Swedish Medical Center board also included enforcing a smoking ban at the hospital. I know it sounds crazy now that doctors, nurses and patients used to be able to smoke inside the hospital at one time but they did.

I got some backlash at the hospital. First we banned smoking in the hospital and then outside near the building. Now it's commonplace not to be allowed to smoke in most public buildings but at that time it was pretty controversial.

I also helped to ban smoking at the Cherry Hills Country Club, where Marlene and I have been members for more than 40 years. The country club, which has hosted the U.S. Masters Golf Championship with the likes of Arnold Palmer and Jack Nicklaus, has a lovely restaurant and clubhouse.

When the smoking ban at Cherry Hills began we got push back from members. But like at Swedish, eventually it became commonplace and members complied. More people also began to learn about the health hazards of second-hand smoke and that helped push for more smoking bans in public buildings, including restaurants and bars.

I didn't know my son, Steve, was a heavy smoker until after his death in 1999. He was an artist and he used his artistic talents on houses. He painted ceilings that looked like marble or the sky or wood and other creative designs. He was enjoying that and making a pretty good living in Hollywood, California, where he lived with his wife.

Steve was healthy as a child even though he was premature. He was always pretty small and thin and was a very picky eater. He'd often be left at the table long after we all finished our meal. As he got older, he got wiser and found a way to sneak his uneaten items into the trash when no one was looking.

His doctors asked us to take him in early to monitor his progress because he was premature and each year he passed the medical tests and grew into an overall healthy adult.

"Steve was a character," his sister, Shari said. "He was in a whole different universe. He was an artist and had a crazy sense of humor. He was one of those people that you wouldn't talk to forever but when you did talk to him it was like you never quit talking to him. He was so present."

When Marlene and I visited Steve and his wife once or twice a year he didn't smoke and we didn't smell it on him. So he was very careful that we didn't know he was smoking. One day he came home from work and told his wife he was tired and going to lay down for awhile. She said his face coloring looked off but thought maybe he just needed rest. She went to check on him 30 minutes later and he was dead. His first heart attack was his last one.

The autopsy found his arteries were all clogged. He was only 47 years old. I suspect his smoking was a major contribution to his death.

Losing Steve was very difficult and it was unusual in my family for men to die at an early age. I come from a line of men who lived to be in their 90s. My father was healthy in his 80s and remarried when he was 87. He lived to be 90. My grandfather Grant, my mother's father, lived to be 94 or 95. He always wore a suit, vest and tie regardless of the weather because that is how he dressed growing up. At age 90 he could still jump high and kick his heels to his buttocks!

Those men were active well into their 80s and that was my goal, too, and exercise and diet played a big role. I believe my healthier lifestyle made it easier for my body to recover from two cancer scares: at 87 years old I was diagnosed with prostate cancer and at 89 doctors discovered I had throat and neck cancer.

The prostate cancer was zapped by radiation and wasn't a major deal. But the throat cancer has had a much longer recovery and it was very scary because of my previous illness with polio. I never got hit with any post-polio symptoms – which hit many polio victims in their later years. Those polio survivors deal with muscle weakness and other symptoms.

But I do think because I already had a weakness in my throat because of the polio the cancer developed there.

Marlene was my caretaker through each cancer scare going with me to the doctors, listening to their treatment plans and keeping a close eye on me at home. Initially, the doctors didn't want to do radiation on my throat because of my age but my overall health convinced them I could handle the treatments.

We spent weeks consulting with several doctors to get a treatment plan and they were aware of my polio illness, although we felt some didn't quite understand the severity of the impact on my throat.

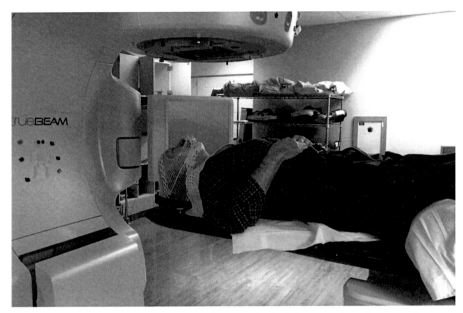

In 2015, I got a shock when doctors discovered I had throat and neck cancer. I went through many months of radiation, which zapped the cancer, but damaged my saliva glands.

I started the treatments and everything was going OK. But one evening I had trouble breathing and ended up in the emergency room. The thing I dreaded the most – another tracheotomy – became necessary because I couldn't breathe without it.

"I know the radiation doctor was in tears when she heard they had to do a tracheotomy," Marlene said. "We called her over when we were in the emergency room and he had trouble breathing that night. She and the surgeon and the doctor on-call all got together and when she first came down she said no to the tracheotomy because she knew his history. But after they all talked, it became clear if he couldn't breathe he wouldn't make it."

At that moment I did question why God had put me in this position again. I had survived polio and now 64 years later I was going through another tracheotomy? I don't wear my religion on my sleeve but I do believe in God and I do say nightly prayers. I also have been a longtime member of the Methodist Church.

As I was working on this book, I discovered a letter my grandfather Wilkins wrote to me in 1936 when I joined the Methodist Church at age 10. Below the Wilkins Bro. Shoe Co. letterhead, it reads:

My Dear Grant,
I have been trying to get time to write to you for several days, but just could not get the time in. Our business has been extra good on white shoes for several days, and we are staying close to catch all we can. I want to congratulate you on joining the Church. It is without doubt the grandest step you will ever take. The Bible says every Tongue shall confess & every knee shall bow. Also he that confesses me before Men him will I confess before my Father who is in Heaven. You have been baptized with the Baptism that your Savior was. He set the example for us to follow. So I congratulate you on taking the step so early in life. You have a long life before you, so you can make it a very useful life if you will. So don't be afraid of working at it. When you get old like I am life will then look very short to you. Don't ever been ashamed of the Gospel of Jesus Christ for it is the power of God unto salvation. God bless you and keep you is my prayer. Kiss your Dear Mother and Dad for me. If you was here I would give you a great big hug. In Love and kisses to all. Bye Bye. Your Loving Grand Dad.
J.C. Wilkins
Your Grand Mother Bess joins me in love to you & all.

I think my grandfather would be very proud of my long membership in the Methodist Church, first at Park Hill Methodist in Denver where Marlene and I were married and the funerals of Diane, our son Steve and my parents took place. When we moved to our new home we joined St. Andrews United Methodist Church. I was chairman of the fundraising committee when we decided to build a larger church and after we raised $275,000 I was chairman of the building committee. Marlene and I also donated a new organ for the new building.

Our new church served about 1,200 members for many years until a new pastor built a larger church in another suburb and our building was sold to another congregation. The building was eventually torn down for senior citizen housing.

PHONE 329   J. C. WILKINS

Wilkins Bros. Shoe Co.

Dealers in Footwear

Mexico, Mo.   5/13/36.

My Dear Grant.

I have been trying to get time to
write to you for several days, but just could not get the
time in. Our bus has been extra good on white shoes for
several days, and we are staying very close ot catch all
we can.

I want to congratulate you on joining the Church.
                        doubt
It is without the grandest step you will ever take.

The Bible says every Tongue shall confess & every knee shall
bow. Also he that confesses me before Men him will I confess
before my Father who is in Heaven.

You have been baptized with the Baptism that your Savior
was. He set the example for us to follow.

So I congatulate you on taking the step so early in life.
You have a long life before you, so you can make it a very
useful life if you will. So dont be afraid of working at
it. When you get old like I am life will then look very short
to you. Dont ever be ashamed of the Gospel of Jesus Christ
for it is the power of God unto salvation.

God bless you and keep you is my prayer.

                        Kiss your Dear
Mother and Dad for me. If you was here I would give you
a great big hug. In Love and kisses to all Bye Bye.

                Your Loving Grand Dad.

your Grand Mother Bess joins me in love to you & all.

I'm grateful I kept a letter my grandfather Wilkins wrote to me in 1936 when I joined
the Methodist Church at age 10.

"We had a really good congregation, with a great mix of people, and we were all neighbors. We had wonderful ministers," Marlene said.

My faith helped me get through my medical challenges and my prayers sustained me during my recovery from throat cancer. I couldn't eat and had to be fed liquids through a tube placed in my stomach. I had to work with a speech therapist to improve my speech and learn how to swallow. The treatments wiped out my saliva glands and saliva is what allows humans to swallow. Slowly, I have been able to reintroduce food but I need to wash it down with water or other liquids because I can't naturally swallow.

Any sympathy I have for myself gets washed away when I go to the CU Cancer Treatment Center and see people much worse than myself. Many cancer victims can't walk or talk. I have to clear my throat often but I can talk and Marlene and I are still taking our daily walks.

I am blessed to have a wife who takes care of my needs, including fighting with insurance companies when they won't cover treatment costs. That is not an easy job!

"Marlene is the quiet one who helps to make it all possible, whether it is helping with his recent illness she is constantly making sure he is where he needs to be," Rotarian John Klug said.

Klug also said I've inspired him to maintain an exercise routine.

"Some nights, I just don't want to walk but then I think of Grant," Klug said.

My children say I am example to them.

"He's just a tough old guy. He just stoically gets up and goes on," Shari said. "That is how he deals with it. Plus, he is fascinated with medical stuff. So he loves doing the research and talking to the people while they are working on him."

Shari survived breast cancer, which we believe was a gene from her mother's side of the family. Her Grandmother Schoelzel and Aunt Laini both had breast cancer.

Mark has been healthy, thank goodness, and says his mother and my health battles also taught him lessons.

"We learned you have to persevere; the whole experience of growing up was a lesson that you do not quit," Mark said. "You had to keep working and figure it out and find a way to make things happens. He is a pretty good example of that."

My children also have influenced me. I learned more about alternative lifestyles from Shari and cringe when I hear people condemn gay people. I sponsored the first gay woman to the Rotary Club of Denver. I asked her to write the introduction so that I would have the right words. When I mentioned she lived with her partner no one batted an eye. We now have several openly gay male and female members and it never has been an issue.

From Mark, I have seen the positive impact of transcendental meditation on his life and admire his work with his students. I even found a local meditation teacher to help me learn to meditate. It is also a joy to see Mark continues to create and sell his pottery, something he began in college. At one time he had a pottery studio in Oregon.

I was proud of Steve, too, and his artistic endeavors. We'll never know what else he would have accomplished in life but while he was here he made his own impact.

Every family has its challenges. Polio has been a big part of all of our lives and helping eradicate it from the world is not only a personal goal but a tribute to all of my family members, who as Shari says, became our village and helped us through our unique challenges.

Afterward

It is a journey in itself to write a memoir. Having spent 90 years on this Earth, I am sure I missed a few things but the main reason for writing the book was to highlight my work with Rotary and especially the importance of polio eradication and childhood immunization.

When I look back, I am proud of my accomplishments as a Rotarian and hope that encourages others to get involved. When I was stricken by polio at age 25, little did I know that my story would play a role in helping to eradicate polio worldwide. I played a small role but a role nevertheless.

I admired my wife, Diane's, courage and positive attitude during her 13 years tied to a respirator and helping to raise our three children. I was so fortunate to have found my second wife, Marlene, who was brave enough to marry a 38-year-old man with three teenagers. She has truly been my partner for more than 50 years.

In 2008, I was named by the Denver Rotary Club "Rotarian of the Year" and we were touched when they surprised us and also named Marlene an honorary member. Women had been allowed membership since 1989 but Marlene never officially joined, even though she had been by my side for all of my Rotary work.

"Everyone probably thought I was already a Rotarian," Marlene joked. "I had the wonderful experience of going to 65 clubs in our district and traveling all over the world with Rotary, visiting hundreds of clubs."

My father introduced me to Rotary and I believe he would be proud of all of the projects I have been involved with since 1969. I am happy I was able to walk in his footsteps and share many Rotary experiences with my brother, Jim.

"When I see someone older whose arm is limp I wonder if they had polio when they were younger," my son, Mark said. "I think my dad's work to eliminate polio is a huge part of his legacy. He hasn't done it by himself, for sure, but he was part of getting the ball rolling and keeps it rolling."

I am fortunate to have had good doctors help care for me during my two cancer scares. As long as I can make a contribution to Rotary, I'll be doing my part.

As we near the end of my story, let's reflect on Rotary International's beginning of the eradication of polio effort and what hopefully will be the end in the near future.

In 1986, there were a reported 350,000 cases of active polio in our world. In 2016, that number had dramatically dropped to only 37 cases; and through mid-April 2017, only five cases have been reported worldwide.

Hopefully, by 2018 we will be able to say there are no more active cases. Then we must go three years without any polio cases in the world before our goal is reached, and WHO can declare our world polio-free.

As I look back over this 31 years of effort, I take comfort that 2.5 billion children worldwide have been immunized against polio, and 16 million children have been saved from paralysis caused by polio.

I had a book mark made that I often passed out at Rotary gatherings. I think it sums up my perception of Rotary and all of the good the organization has done worldwide. I wrote it before women were allowed to join but please know the "he" is also a "she" in the below. I think it is a good way to end this book.

What is a Rotarian?

A Rotarian is a person who digs wells from which he won't drink.

A person who vaccinates children he will never meet;

Who restores eyesight for those he won't ever see;

Who builds housing he will never live in;

Who educates children he will never know;

Who plants trees he will never see or sit under;

Who feeds hungry people, regardless of color, race or politics;

Who makes crawlers into walkers halfway around the world;

Who knows real happiness, which as Albert Schweitzer said,
"can only be found by serving others."

I would like to thank Cindy Brovsky, a former newspaper journalist, for helping me write this book. Cindy understands the impact polio has on families because her mother, Marie I. Brovsky, was stricken at the age of 16.

Grant Wilkins Service in Rotary

- 1969 – Joined Rotary Club of Denver, Club 31
- 1974, 1976, 1993 & 2001 – Denver Rotary Club Silver Dollar Awards
- 1978-1979 – Rotary Club of Denver, president
- 1981 – First Artists of America, chairman; annual event ran through 2000 and raised more than $3 million for Denver Rotary Foundation and Colorado History Museum.
- 1984-1985 – Rotary International Governor of District 5450
- 1984-1985 – New Club Awards (3) from RI President Carlos Conseco "Discover a New World of Service
- 1984-1985 – Citation for Meritorious service from RI
- 1984 – Artists of America, chairman, appreciation from Denver Rotary Club with Glenna Goodacre, artist bronze
- 1985 – Artists of America, chairman, appreciation from DRC with Kent Ullberg, artist bronze
- 1985 – Artists of America, chairman emeritus (five years of service) "A Lion of a Man"
- 1986-1987 – Distinguished Service Award, Trustees of Rotary International
- 1990 – Honolulu Rotary International Zone Institute, associate chairman (Richard King, director)
- 1993-1995 – Rotary International Director
- 1993 – International Director, Aspen Rotary International Zone Institute – Bronze
- 1994 – International Director, Seattle Rotary International Zone Institute – Bronze
- 1994-1995 – Rotarian of the Year, Rotary District 5450
- 1996-1997 – International Award for Polio-Free World, RI Foundation (Rajendra K. Saboo, RI President)
- 2002 – RI President's Personal Representative, Russia's 1st Rotary District Conference, St. Petersburg, Russia.
- 2008-2009 – Rotarian of the Year (Denver Rotary Club), Plastic Square with 2008 Silver Dollar
- 2008-2009 – Rotary Service Above Self Award (RI President D.K. Lee), given to only 150 Rotarians annually

- 2010-2013 – Denver Rotary Club, member Board of Directors
- Rotary International Finance Committee, chairman for one year
- Rotary International Health & Hunger Task Force
- Rotary International Audit & Operations Review Committee, three-year term
- Rotary International Health Initiative, chairman of task force for several years
- Rotary International Chairman 1st Russian Peace Conference, Anchorage, Alaska
- Rotary International Co-chairman 2nd Russian Peace Conference , St. Petersburg, Russia
- Board member on the original U.S.C.B. (United States, Canada and Bermuda) PolioPlus Committee; involved in fundraising since 1985, giving speeches to promote the eradication of polio worldwide, advocacy with U.S. Congress and history review
- Represented Rotary International and PolioPlus at a National Immunization Day in the Ivory Coast along with his wife, Marlene
- Rotary International's PolioPlus bronze statues. He arranged with world famous artist Glenna Goodacre to design a larger-than-life bronze statue depicting a Rotarian helping to vaccine children worldwide for polio. He also arranged for Richard Gooding, a Denver Rotary member who owned and operated a foundry, to donate one statute for Rotary International headquarters in Evanston, Illinois and another at the Colorado University Medical Center campus in Aurora, Colorado.
- Consultant Rotary International Foundation
- Rotary International president's representative to numerous district conferences in dozens of countries and many U.S. states
- Rotary's representative to the Library of Congress in the formation of the Russian Leadership program, now called Open World.
- 2006 Open World Award along with Rotarian Carolyn Jones

Grant Wilkins Civic Activities
- National City Bank, Board of Directors
- Mesa Verde National Park Foundation, Board of Directors
- Heard Museum in Phoenix, Board of Directors of the Heard Foundation
- Millicent Rogers Museum, Taos, N.M., Board of Directors
- Colorado History Museum, Board of Directors and Trustee
- Common Ground, Board of Directors
- Children's Hospital Foundation, Board of Directors
- National Roadside Business Association (N.R.B.A), trade association for outdoor advertising, President
- St. Andrew United Methodist Church, fundraising chairman and building committee chairman
- Warren & Sommer Insurance Agency, Board of Directors
- Beehive International, Salt Lake City (manufacturing plant in Ireland), Board of Directors, 2010-2013
- Chancellors Society, University of Denver, donors giving at least $2,000 annually to D.U., chair Grant Wilkins Honors/Miscellaneous Awards
- 2015 Humanitarian of the Year – given annually by the University of Denver's Korbel School of International Studies to outstanding humanitarian. Previous winners include former President George W. Bush.
- 2013 - "Daniel L. Ritchie Award" – given annually by the Colorado Ethics in Business Association to an outstanding business person. University of Colorado at Colorado Spring students interviewed about 100 people for the award.
- 2004 - Beta Theta Pi (Alpha Zeta) Hall of Fame inductee at University of Denver
- 1986-1988 - Appreciation Award Children's Health Corp. & Child Health Management Services, Inc.
- 1986 – Community Service Award, Founders Day, March 17, 1986, University of Denver Alumni Association
- 1983-1987 – Colorado Highway Commissioner, appointed by Governors Richard Lamm and Roy Romer

• 1970-1990 – Swedish Medical Center (Englewood, Colorado), Board of Trustees for 20 years; Chairman of the foundation for one year; and President of the board for three years
• 1943 – First Boy Scout in Louisiana to receive the Gold, Silver & Bronze Palm awards to go on Eagle Scout Badge
• 1942 – Boy Scouts of America Eagle Scout Award, Lafayette, Louisiana – Troop #19

I will be forever grateful to my parents (middle sitting) and my brother, Jim, (left with his first wife, Joey) for their love and support. We gathered in this photo while celebrating my parent's 60th wedding anniversary. They helped me raise my children after Diane was stricken with polio and welcomed Marlene into the family.

I can think of no better way to have celebrated my 90th birthday on Oct. 23, 2016 than to be with Marlene, my children, grandchildren and great-grandchildren. Their love and support helped me overcome health obstacles and their encouragement allowed me to follow my dreams of being involved with Rotary. (l. to r.) Grand-daughter Tahra; Grandson Newlin, wife Hallie and baby Celeste; Son Mark and wife JoAnne; Neil Rever and wife Bonnie (widow of our deceased son, Steve); Grandson Benjamin, wife Josephine and son Teddy, and daughter Shari.

Made in the USA
San Bernardino, CA
15 September 2017